All-in-One Guide to
Cake Decorating

Janice Murfitt

3 9082 12758 1935

All-in-One Guide to Cake Decorating

CompanionHouse Books™ is an imprint of Fox Chapel Publishers International Ltd.

Project Team
Editorial Director: Christopher Reggio
Editor: Amy Deputato
Technical Editor: Dolores York
Copy Editor: Laura Taylor
Design: Mary Ann Kahn
Index: Elizabeth Walker

ISBN 978-1-62008-240-9

Library of Congress Cataloging-in-Publication Data
Names: Murfitt, Janice, author.
Title: All-in-one guide to cake decorating : over 100 step-by-step cake
    decorating techniques and recipes / Janice Murfitt.
Description: Mount Joy, PA : Fox Chapel Publishers International Ltd., 2017.
    | Includes index.
Identifiers: LCCN 2017027305| ISBN 9781620082409 (softcover) | ISBN
    9781620082416 (eISBN)
Subjects: LCSH: Cake decorating. | LCGFT: Cookbooks.
Classification: LCC TX771.2 .M868 2017 | DDC 641.86/539--dc23
LC record available at https://lccn.loc.gov/2017027305

This book has been published with the intent to provide accurate and authoritative information in regard to the subject matter within. While every precaution has been taken in the preparation of this book, the author and publisher expressly disclaim any responsibility for any errors, omissions, or adverse effects arising from the use or application of the information contained herein.

Fox Chapel Publishing
903 Square Street
Mount Joy, PA 17552

Fox Chapel Publishers International Ltd.
7 Danefield Road, Selsey (Chichester)
West Sussex PO20 9DA, U.K.

www.facebook.com/companionhousebooks

Printed and bound in Singapore
20 19 18 17   2 4 6 8 10 9 7 5 3 1

Contents

Introduction

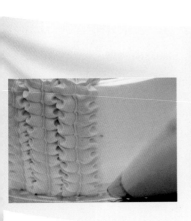

he first steps in cake decorating are always the most important. Once you've perfected the basics, they will give you not only a good foundation of skills but also the confidence and experience to master the more advanced techniques of this craft.

With clear techniques to follow, this book teaches cake making, icing, and decorating so it's fun to do and learn. The fully illustrated chapters take you through the basic techniques step by step and include choosing the right equipment, planning cake designs, and making templates.

Creating cakes that are worthy of decoration is as important as the icing and decorating. A chapter is devoted to the simple steps for shaping and cutting, filling, and layering, which gives you a wide variety of cakes to choose from. This leads to a chapter on more complex special occasion cakes that details how to cover cakes with marzipan, fondant, and royal icing for a professional finish. Methods for round, square, and unusually shaped cakes with various finishes are also presented.

You'll learn how to choose and use different kinds of food coloring with a variety of icing types. By carefully selecting the right ingredients, you can create amazing effects.

No cake-decorating book would be complete without a chapter on chocolate! Who can resist the smooth, velvety finish of a cake covered with chocolate curls, chocolate leaves, or chocolate-dipped fruit?

Other sections of the book cover more advanced work, such as using fondant for frills, cutouts, and extension pieces as well as modeling decorative objects and figures. We'll discuss the many different ways that you can decorate cakes with piped designs, including delicate line work, run-outs, embroidery, flowers, and motifs. Gum paste is a wonderful icing medium for making all types of simple flowers, molded flowers, cutouts, and wired flower sprays. With care and practice, you'll be able to use these methods to reproduce flowers with stunning and realistic results.

The recipes at the end of the book have been tested and are proven to give consistently good results. You'll also find helpful cake-making and icing tips throughout the book.

I hope this book gives you much enjoyment and inspires you with many ideas for creative and delicious cakes. By following the steps presented herein, you will perfect the techniques and achieve the attractive and professional-looking results that every cake decorator desires.

Getting Started

ith any craft, cake decorating included, there are basic principles that will help ensure successful results every time. First, using good-quality equipment and materials is a must, and here you will find sound advice for choosing and buying the essentials. In addition, a beautiful cake doesn't just materialize; for the best results, you will need to plan your cake designs in detail from the cake base to the most subtle of decorative touches. This chapter will serve as a useful starting point to help you plan a cake that will perfectly suit the person or occasion for which you are making it.

Cake-Icing Equipment

For the very best results when icing cakes, you must have the right tools. Although a vast selection of equipment is available from various outlets, it is best to purchase from specialty cake-decorating retailers. You may pay more for the professional equipment sold by such stores, but the higher quality will help you produce the results you desire. The best equipment, carefully used and stored, will last for a very long time and may never need to be replaced, thus paying for itself several times over in its lifetime.

Although there are many companies that sell cake-decorating equipment online, beginners should look at tools in person before actually buying them. Start with the following essentials:

- acrylic board
- acrylic rolling pin
- crimpers
- icing smoother
- icing spatula
- icing tubes (a small selection)
- patterned side scraper
- straight side scraper
- turntable

These items will enable you to use royal icing or fondant and crimp or pipe a design. As your cake-icing skills improve, you can purchase more equipment as you need it and quickly build up a good "toolbox."

You must always use, wash, and store your cake-icing equipment very carefully to avoid damage and to ensure that it lasts. Keep all of your implements together in a spotlessly clean, dry place away from any cold or damp areas. Store icing tubes in a box specially designed to keep them upright; this will prevent the ends from being damaged (it will also allow you to easily find the one you need at a glance). Always clean the tubes with a tube brush specially designed to clean the pointed ends without damaging them. Thoroughly dry all equipment—tubes, crimpers, cutters, pans, and anything else made of metal—to prevent rust and discoloration that, in turn, can stain future icing or sugar work. Here are more useful tips:

- Store acrylic or plastic boards flat in a dry place to prevent them from warping or being scratched. Scratched acrylic or plastic surfaces harbor dirt and may impart impurities to your sugar work.
- Wash and dry canvas piping bags thoroughly. Damp items will encourage discoloration and the growth of mold.
- Store straight edges and side scrapers carefully to prevent any damage to their surfaces; otherwise, this will affect the smoothness of the icing.
- Have your scale checked and serviced regularly to ensure that it accurately measures ingredients.

Special Equipment for Icing

Acrylic rolling pin and board

These tools may be expensive, but they provide nonstick surfaces and are easy to clean, practical to use, and available in a variety of sizes. Use them for rolling out small pieces of fondant or marzipan for decorations.

Acrylic skewers

Skewers support the tiers of fondant-covered cakes. They clean up easily and can be cut to size before being covered with the cake pillars.

Brushes

Fine artists' brushes, available in different sizes, have many uses for painting flowers and sugar plaques with food coloring; they are also useful when making icing run-outs.

Cake board

Often made of corrugated cardboard or another stiff material, cake boards serve as a base on which cakes are decorated, lifted, stacked, and transported.

Cake pillars

Plastic pillars may be round, square, or octagonal and usually have a hole through the center so you can place them over acrylic skewers to support tiered cakes (for example, fondant-covered wedding cakes).

Cheesecloth

Cheesecloth is used for covering royal icing to prevent a skin from forming; because cheesecloth is white, it will not discolor the icing. Keep the cheesecloth clean and dry while in storage.

Crimpers

Crimpers come in a variety of shapes and sizes and offer many different patterns. You may purchase them in sets or individually.

Dowels

Dowels in different thicknesses are useful for holding drying leaves and petals to give them more realistic, curved shapes.

Floral tape

Tape, often seen in shades of green, used by florists to tape stems together or cover floral wire.

Floral wire

Wire comes in various gauges and colors for wiring sugar flowers onto stems and for making floral sprays.

Flower nail

You can make your own with a wine cork and a large nail or you can buy one from a kitchen store or cake-decorating specialist. Flower nails are invaluable when piping flowers.

Icing smoother
Use this essential tool to smooth fondant to a flawless, glossy finish.

Icing syringe
Ideal for simple piping, icing syringes usually come with a selection of tubes.

Icing-tube brush
A necessary tool for cleaning icing tubes without bending or distorting the ends.

Icing tubes
Straight-sided metal tubes are the best because they produce clean, sharp results and they fit into parchment-paper piping bags. They are available in a range of different designs and sizes and are ideal for piping cream, meringues, and buttercream frosting.

Piping bags
Piping bags are made in a variety of materials. Nylon piping bags are soft and flexible, making them suitable for cream, meringue, and icing. Buy small, medium, and large piping bags. You can also make your own from parchment paper and a variety of straight-sided tubes or even without a tube.

Side scrapers
Side scrapers are made from plastic or stainless steel and are used for smoothing icing on the sides of a cake. The plastic versions are more flexible and easier to use. Patterned side scrapers come in a variety of designs and are ideal for finishing the sides of a cake with different designs.

Small cutters
These are used for cutting out various shapes, numbers, and letters in fondant, marzipan, chocolate, or fruit zest to use as decorations. Tiny specialty cutters are available for making cutout flowers from fondant and marzipan.

Stamens
Stamens come in different colors and finishes from cake-decorating retailers and are used in the center of molded and cutout sugar flowers.

Straight edge
A good straight edge is rigid and will not scratch or bend when used on top of a cake to obtain flat, smooth icing. Straight edges are available in various lengths; as a general rule, a 12-inch (30-cm) straight edge is easier to handle on cakes up to 10 inches (25 cm) in size. Those made from stainless steel are best.

Turntable
This is the most essential piece of equipment for easy movement of cakes while icing and decorating. Check that the turntable is stable and make sure it revolves smoothly. Buy the best quality you can afford.

Tweezers
Tweezers with rounded ends are indispensable for delicate work.

Cake-Icing Equipment: 1. Acrylic rolling pin, 2. Acrylic board, 3. Icing smoother, 4. Floral wires in various gauges and colors, 5. Patterned and plain side scrapers in plastic and stainless steel, 6. Icing-tube brush, 7. Fine straight-sided metal tubes in a variety of sizes and designs, 8. Parchment-paper piping bags, 9. Floral tape, 10. Stamens, 11. Turntable, 12. Garret frill cutter, 13. Fluted cutter, 14. Cutting knife, 15. Rounded-end tweezers, 16. Crimpers, 17. Small scissors, 18. Scribing tool, 19. Modeling tools, 20. Acrylic skewers, 21. Flower nail, 22. Flower cutters, 23. Artists' brushes, 24. Stainless-steel straight edge, 25. Small cutters, 26. Large piping tubes, 27. Nylon piping bag

Initial Planning

Before starting to make a cake for a special occasion, think through the whole idea and plan every detail carefully. Don't rush into it with little thought of the final shape, size, or finish. There are many factors to consider in the planning stages, before you even buy the ingredients.

- The occasion for which you are making the cake, such as a birthday, wedding, baptism, or anniversary. This plays a big role in the type of cake you will make.
- The person for whom you're making the cake. Consider the recipient's age and sex as well as any particular interests, skills, or hobbies that can influence the design and theme of the cake.
- The required ingredients to make the cake. Chocolate or vanilla? A light sponge cake or a rich fruit cake? There are many options.
- The shape and size of the cake. Round, square, oval, horseshoe, heart, flower...the list

goes on. You may need specially shaped pans, which you can buy or possibly even rent from a supplier or bakery. You'll need cake boards of the corresponding shapes and sizes, too.

- The design of the cake. The design is always a personal aspect of cake decorating, and we all know our strong points and favorite techniques. It's not sensible to attempt aspects of sugarcraft in which you are not experienced.
- How much time you have available to make and decorate the cake. The time factor can also affect your choice of design. If you are short on time, it's better to make a simple, well-finished cake rather than an intricate cake that may be ruined by rushing at the last minute.
- The color scheme and type of icing required. Does the event already have a color scheme? If possible, try to acquire samples of the fabric, flowers, or ribbons to use as a guide when choosing icing colors as well as colors for the cake's decorations.
- The cake's final destination and how you will transport it if necessary. Avoid fragile decorations, like extension work, for a cake that has to travel a long distance because any breakage will spoil the design.

Once you have considered all of these factors, you can confidently begin to create detailed plans for your cake.

Cake Designing

A cake designed for a special event is often the centerpiece of the occasion. Prominently displayed, it will be viewed from all angles, so you must plan the design and decorations with this in mind.

Once you've decided on the shape and size of the cake, you can plan your design. The base color of the cake has a strong impact on the finished design. White, champagne, or pastel shades are the safest colors to choose for special-occasion cakes, but bolder colors may be appropriate for children's cakes or novelty designs.

When it comes to the base covering, there are three main choices: (1) the clean, sharp, classic lines of royal icing; (2) the rounded, smooth finish of fondant; or (3) the softer effect of a buttercream-frosted finish. The covering dramatically affects the appearance of the cake as well as your decoration choices. Run-outs, also known as floodwork, look wonderful on a royal-iced cake, just as frills and flounces look perfect on a fondant cake, and instant decorations, such as crushed

Cake Designing

The inspiration for this cake design was a remnant of upholstery fabric. The fabric design was simplified to make the pieces easier to cut out of fondant. The design was drawn on tracing paper to provide a template and then each piece of the design was cut out separately and applied to the dry fondant cake. To ensure an accurate fit of all the pieces, they were arranged while still pliable and then pressed lightly into position.

Design Inspiration

Each of the items shown here has a design, pattern, or print that you could use when planning a cake design. Lace designs may be used to make piped lace pieces; pieces of embroidery or embroidery transfer designs can form the basis of a piped design. Designs on china can inspire border piping or eyelet-lace work. Fabrics, wallpapers, and greetings cards offer bold prints that you may adapt for run-outs, cutouts, or motifs for sugar plaques or food-coloring pen designs.

nuts, candied fruit, and sugar-frosted flowers, complement frosted creations.

If you need some inspiration for the design, look at fabric and wallpaper books, china or ceramic pieces, or embroidery patterns for designs that you can re-create in icing. Look at photographs of cakes to find appealing designs to which you can add your own personal touches. Don't be afraid to mix and match ideas and techniques. Simple methods presented in this book include ribbons, embossing, and crimping. As your skills improve, you can move on to run-out motifs and letters, ribbon insertion, collars and corner pieces, and piped work, all of which require precise templates before embarking on the design. You'll need to employ a bit of math along with careful measuring and cutting; accuracy is the most important factor.

Making and Using Templates

Templates are very useful for inscribing shapes and designs on the tops and sides of cakes. Always keep the templates that you make. Label them with the cake size so you can reuse them; you may even be able to adapt round templates for square cakes. Following are some examples of how you can make your own templates. For ready-made templates that you can adapt for your own use, see pages 213-217.

Top Templates

To make a top template for a circular cake, trace a paper circle that is the same size as the cake's diameter and then cut away about 1 inch (2.5 cm) all around the circle. Fold the circle in half and then in half twice more to make eight sections. Alternatively, fold the circle in half and then fold this semicircle in three to make six sections. Either way, you will always end up with a cone shape.

To make a scalloped template, place a suitable round object at the base of the cone, draw a pencil line around the shape, and carefully cut it out. When you open up the template, the edge will be scalloped. To adapt this design, place the round object halfway over the end of the cone shape and draw around the shape, rounding the curve inward instead of outward. You may also apply this technique to a square template.

To use the template, hold it gently on top of the cake and draw around it with a scribing tool. You can then pipe over the outline and fill in the shape with trellis or cornelli work (see pages 149 and 150).

How to Make a Top Template

1. Cut out a circle of paper to the diameter of the cake, then trim about 1 inch (2.5 cm) all around.
2. Fold the circle to make eight sections and then position a round object, such as a cup, so that the rim touches the base of the cone. Draw around the cup to form a curve.
3. Cut out the round outline to form a scalloped template. Alternatively, draw and cut out an inverted curve on the base of the cone using a small plate or saucer.
4. To transfer the design to the top of the cake, center the template on the cake and draw around it with a scribing tool.

Side Templates

To make a side template, cut a piece of parchment paper to the exact height and circumference of the cake. Make sure that the strip of paper fits accurately around the cake before you begin making the template. If you are making frills to decorate the cake's sides, you will need a template to determine exactly where you will apply the frills. Fold the side template into as many sections as there are to be frills around the cake. Place a round object halfway over the base of the folded template and draw around it with a pencil to make a scalloped edge. Cut the template out, affix to the cake, and scribe the scalloped drops to make the frill spacing or to use as a guide for piping dropped-loop thread work.

How to Make a Side Template

1. Cut a paper template to the exact height and circumference of the cake. To form a scalloped side template for spacing frills or for a scalloped piping design, fold the strip into as many sections as you need.
2. Draw around a cup or other suitable round object to form an inverted curve and cut carefully around the outline.
3. Fix the template to the cake and follow the scalloped outline with a scribing tool. You can use the marked "drops" for positioning fondant frills or as a guide for piping work.

Other Templates

Run-out templates: Because cakes vary in size, sometimes even just slightly, you will have to design a new run-out collar template for each cake you are decorating. First, measure the top of the cake and replicate it on a paper template. Add the collar design to the template, allowing 2 inches (5 cm) all around the template to incorporate the design. Popular designs include inward and outward scallops and hexagonal, round, and square shapes.

Ribbon-insertion templates: For ribbon insertion, the template must fit the top and sides of the cake. Accurately draw two lines the width of the ribbon and mark the spaces where you will insert the ribbon. You can use straight or curved lines, but make sure that the lines are evenly spaced; otherwise, when you transfer the design to the cake, the ribbon pieces will look uneven.

Shaping, Filling, and Simple Icings

Chapter 2

ith a little imagination and a few simple techniques, you can completely transform everyday cakes. If you cannot find a cake pan in the shape you want, you can cut and shape a cake to form simple geometric and curved shapes or more ambitious novelty designs. There are also different methods for slicing and layering cakes together with a variety of delicious fillings to produce attractive effects once the cake is cut. Finally, there are many types of icings and frostings to produce smooth finishes or patterned effects.

Shaping Cakes

With some careful cutting and shaping, you can make many shapes from simple round or square cakes: animals, numbers, flowers, cars, and many others. Sometimes you will need to cut several required shapes out of a larger cake, or you can bake and shape several cakes and assemble them to create the desired end result. Most types of cake can be shaped, but a cake made from a cake mix, any flavor or color, is the most reliable.

When you are ready to shape the cake(s), figure out exactly how you need to cut to form the desired shape(s). Measurements can be crucial to the end result, so measure and mark the cake(s) and then cut the pieces carefully with a sharp, straight-bladed knife to make clean cuts. You can also use cookie cutters as needed because they also make good, clean shapes, which will make assembling the pieces easier.

"Crumb-coat" your cake by spreading a thin layer of frosting on all pieces or brushing all pieces lightly with apricot glaze (see page 205) and letting them dry. This crumb coat will catch any crumbs from the cut sides of the cake, thus preventing them from getting into the outer layer of icing.

Assemble the pieces using apricot glaze, icing, or frosting to help you form the pieces into the intended shape. Once assembled, place the cake on a cake board so that you do not have to handle it any more than is necessary.

At this stage, you are ready to cover the cake with fondant, marzipan, icing, or buttercream frosting. Pay attention to maintaining the proper shape throughout the finishing process.

Did You Know?

Cutting and shaping is always easier on a cake that has been given ample time to settle, about two or three days.

Simple Shaping

Simply cutting round or square cakes can create a wide variety of shapes. For example, by cutting a square cake in half diagonally and placing the resulting triangles back to back, you have a diamond-shaped cake. Here are some other ideas.

How to Make the Letter Z

1. Cut a square cake in half diagonally to form two triangles. Slide one half down along the cut until it touches the other half for only about 4 inches (10 cm), producing a Z shape.
2. Crumb-coat the two pieces and brush the joint with apricot glaze (see page 205), frosting, or icing to assemble.
3. For a quick and easy finish, cover the cake with a flavored buttercream frosting or other icing and decorate as desired.

1   2   3

1

2

3

How to Make the Letter S

1. Cut a round cake in half and slide one half down along the cut until it resembles an S shape.
2. Crumb-coat the two pieces and brush the joint with apricot glaze, frosting, or icing to assemble.
3. When smoothly coated with fondant, this makes an attractive and ideal special-occasion cake for someone whose name begins with "S."

1

How to Cut Slab Cakes into Shapes

1. Bake a cake in a 10 × 8 × 1½-inch (25 × 20 × 4-cm) pan so that the cake is about 1 inch (2.5 cm) deep. Using simple round and oval cookie cutters, make shapes by pressing the cutters directly onto the cake to cut the pieces out cleanly.
2. To cut the cake into triangles, squares, rectangles, and the like, simply measure the shape carefully and cut.
3. Seal the edges of your shapes with a crumb-coat of apricot glaze, frosting, or icing. Cover the shapes with royal icing and decorate with simple decorations.

2

Checkered Cake
Deceptively simple on the outside, this cake reveals a surprise to the person who cuts it.

1

2

3

How to Make a Checkered Cake

1. Make two 7-inch (18-cm) round cakes in contrasting colors, such as chocolate and vanilla. Using a plain pastry cutter with a 2-inch (5-cm) diameter, carefully cut out a small round from the center of each cake. Then use a similar cutter with a diameter of 4 inches (10 cm) to cut out a further central ring from each cake.
2. Replace the cutout pieces of cake, switching the rings of each cake with that of the contrasting color, chocolate for vanilla and vanilla for chocolate. Brush each piece with apricot glaze before reassembling the cakes.
3. Place one cake on top of the other.
4. Finish with chocolate and vanilla buttercream frosting. Coat the sides with grated chocolate, and pipe the top with contrasting buttercream-frosting stars. When the cake is sliced, it will reveal a perfectly checkered pattern.

Did You Know?
If you are making layers by cutting across an oblong cake, measure accurately before cutting. Remember the old saying "measure twice, cut once."

Making Numeral Cakes

You can easily make numeral shapes from round, square, or oblong cake bases. Draw the desired number on paper and use it as a template for cutting out the entire number or pieces that you will assemble to make the number. If you want your numbers to have square instead of round edges, cut them from a 13 × 9-inch (33 × 23-cm) rectangular cake.

How to Make a Number 3 Cake

1. To make the number 3, either bake two 7-inch (18-cm) round cakes or use two ring molds of the same size to bake two Bundt cakes. If you bake two round cakes, use a 3-inch (7.5-cm) plain cutter to remove a round from the center of each. Cut one-third away from each of the rings of cake.
2. Position the two cutout cakes as shown and cut away the excess so that the two pieces join together to make a 3.
3. When you are happy with how it looks, crumb-coat the whole cake with apricot glaze, frosting, or icing and allow it to set before covering the entire cake with buttercream frosting or other icing and then decorating.

1

2

Number 3 Cake

The smooth buttercream frosting on this fun birthday cake is simply decorated with cornelli work (see page 150) piped from a plain writing tube. You can finish the decoration with brightly colored candies and decorate the cake board with sprinkles.

Tractor Cake

To cover and decorate the tractor, spread all of the cake pieces with colored icing and reassemble, pressing together well. Spread pairs of large round cookies sandwiched together with buttercream frosting for the back wheels and repeat with smaller cookies for the front wheels. Trim the cabin, the engine grille, and the wheels with licorice strips and use hard candies for the wheel trim and headlights.

Designer Novelty Cakes

When designing and making novelty cakes, careful planning is vital. Figure out the components of your selected design on paper and then decide what size and shape of cake or cakes will be needed. Trial and error is sometimes the only way to get the cake you envision, but that is part of the fun.

How Make a Tractor Cake

1. Bake a cake in a 2-pound (1-kg) loaf pan. Cut a 2-inch (5-cm) piece off each end of the cake.
2. Trim one end piece to match the thickness of a mini chocolate-covered jelly roll. Brush all of the pieces with apricot glaze.
3. To assemble the cake, position the mini jelly roll crosswise on one side of the cake board with the trimmed-off piece at right angles to it to support the cabin. Arrange the cabin and engine housing on the supports to ensure that all pieces fit neatly.

1

2

3

Making Layer Cakes

It's fun to cut into a layer cake and reveal its many layers and fillings; you can even incorporate a variety of flavors into the same cake. The options can be endless—for example, alternating chocolate layers with vanilla, orange, lemon, and lime, or layering plain sponge cake with chocolate and coffee fillings to give sharp contrast in appearance and flavor.

It can be tricky to make a cake with perfect layers, but there are many ways to achieve the desired end result. You can make a deep cake in a single pan and cut it carefully into three layers. You can bake two cakes of the same size and cut each into two layers, resulting in a total of four layers. If you want a cake with many thin layers, you must bake the layers on baking sheets. An interesting twist on a layer cake is to bake a Genoese sponge cake in a jelly roll pan, cut it across into three rectangular strips, and layer the strips to form an oblong-shaped cake.

Use the following tips for layer-cake success:
* Bake evenly sized cakes with level tops so the layers will be flat when you assemble the cake. Be sure to level out the mixture in the pans before baking.

Did You Know?

Always lift and position each layer carefully on top of the other, supporting it with the palms of both hands. Check that the cake is level after adding each new layer so that it does not look uneven when finished.

- Use good-quality baking pans.
- Prepare your baking pans properly; if using a cake mix, read the instructions. Some cake mixes require fully lined pans while others need only to be lightly greased and dusted with flour.
- If you need to divide a cake mix between more than one pan, split the mixture evenly and then weigh the pans on scales to make sure.
- If you are baking thin layers on baking sheets, first line the sheets with parchment paper and then draw the outline of each layer. Spread the mixture to just inside the marked lines.
- Ensure that the oven racks are level so that the cakes bake evenly.

Once you've baked and cooled the cakes, cut them into layers if necessary. To do so, place a cake on a thin cake board on a turntable at eye level. Using a long, sharp knife, make evenly spaced marks on the side of the cake for the number of layers you need. Cut into the side of the cake in a sawing motion as you slowly revolve the cake, keeping the cut level. You may find this easier if you hold a thin cake board on top of the cake to keep it steady. Once you have cut all around the side of the cake, continue the sawing motion to separate the layers. Repeat to cut more layers if necessary.

Frosting or Icing?

The terms *frosting* and *icing* are often used interchangeably (as I do in this book) to describe the coating that covers cakes and other baked goods.

Frosting is a thick, usually fluffy, mixture that can be cooked or uncooked and is often flavored with chocolate or other flavorings. Used for coating or filling cakes, frostings range from quickly swirled meringues to more fluid types, such as buttercream.

Icing is a thin, sugary coating that usually hardens on cooling. Icings are generally thinner and glossier than frostings and are used to coat the outside of cakes.

How to Layer Two Cakes Together

1. Make an 8-inch (20-cm) round chocolate cake and an 8-inch (20-cm) round white cake. Use a turntable and a sharp knife to cut each cake into two even layers.
2. Spread a base layer of white cake evenly with buttercream filling. Arrange a layer of chocolate cake on top and spread it with buttercream filling.
3. Repeat alternating layers of cake and filling until all are sandwiched in position.
4. Chill the cake to retain its shape and then finish the cake by coating it with the remaining buttercream.

1

2

3

How to Layer an Oblong Cake

1. Make a sponge cake in a 13 × 9-inch (33 × 23-cm) jelly-roll pan. Measure the cake carefully and cut it into three equal strips. Roll out a piece of marzipan very thinly and cut it into three pieces to match the cake layers.

2. Brush one layer of cake with warmed jam or jelly and then top with a layer of marzipan. Spread the marzipan with cold chocolate icing.

3. Repeat the process with another layer of cake brushed with jelly and a layer of marzipan and chocolate icing.

4. Top with the last cake layer, jam, and marzipan.

5. Roll out a thin length of marzipan to fit around the sides of the cake. Brush it with jam and fit it smoothly into position.

6. Allow the marzipan to set and then finish by coating the cake with the remaining chocolate icing.

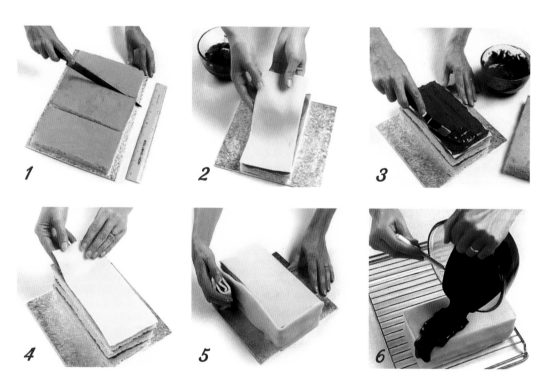

Thinner Frostings and Icings

Covering cakes with frosting gives you a choice of a smooth surface or a textured finish. If you want a smooth finish, keep the cake on a thin cake board that is the same size as the cake or slightly smaller, and place it on a cooling rack over a plate on a turntable.

Make the frosting to the correct consistency; it should be thick enough to coat the back of a spoon evenly. If it is too thick, place the bowl over hot water to melt the frosting (it will still be warm at this stage) or add a little water. If the frosting is too thin, allow it to cool so that it thickens.

Before actually frosting the cake, make sure you have an icing spatula ready. Pour the frosting over the cake and allow it to fall freely over the sides. Resist the temptation to spread the frosting; rather, gently tap or shake the cake to encourage the frosting to fall evenly from the top.

Once the frosting has stopped falling, run your icing spatula around the base of the cake board to neaten the edge, and then allow the covering to dry. Carefully transfer the cake to a cake plate before adding the finishing touches.

If you want a cake with a really sharp and defined shape, first spread some of the frosting over the cake to coat it evenly. Then, using a wet icing spatula, spread the frosting as smoothly as possible to shape it. Allow this first coat of frosting to set before you pour the remaining frosting over the cake as previously described.

Royal Icing Small Cakes

1. You may pour royal icing directly over small cakes, providing you have already crumb-coated them (see page 25). For a very smooth finish, add a very thin layer of marzipan over the cakes before icing them. You may also place small marzipan shapes on top of the cakes for decoration.

2. Make your royal icing to the correct consistency; it should be thick enough to coat the back of a spoon with a transparent coat of icing that does not run off.

3. Place the cakes, spaced apart, on small cake boards on a cooling rack over a tray, plate, or sheet of parchment paper.

4. Using an angled icing spatula to lift and support each cake, spoon the icing over the cake in one movement.

5. Once you've coated all of the cakes, leave them in position to dry. Carefully remove the icing from underneath the cakes before removing them from the cooling rack.

Did You Know?

Once royal icing has set, it has a tendency to crack when the cake is moved. It is therefore important to place the cake on a plate or board before icing it.

3   **4**

How to Make Chocolate Frosting with a Smooth Finish

1. Place the cake on a wire rack over a baking tray or on a plate set on a turntable.
2. Make the chocolate frosting, ensuring that it is the right consistency to coat the back of a spoon.
3. Pour the frosting quickly over the cake to coat completely.
4. Shake the tray gently to encourage the frosting to cover the cake evenly and smoothly; use an angled icing spatula to smooth the surface, if necessary.
5. When the excess frosting has stopped falling, carefully place the cake on a plate or a board. Allow the frosting to set completely before decorating the top and/or sides.

How to Feather Icing

1. Make the royal icing to the correct consistency, so that it is thick enough to coat the back of a spoon without running off.
2. Tint one-quarter of the icing a different color and place it in a parchment-paper piping bag; fold down the top and have a pair of scissors ready.
3. Place your cake on a cake board and pour the remaining icing over the top of the cake. Working fairly quickly, coax it to the edge of the cake with a paintbrush to make the icing even.
4. Snip the point off the piping bag and pipe parallel lines of icing across the top of the cake.
5. Drag a toothpick across the lines of icing in one direction and then in the opposite direction to create a feathered effect. Allow the icing to set.

Citrus Petal Cake

A light sponge cake filled with fresh
whipped cream and coated in lightly
toasted flaked almonds. The top is piped
with whipped cream swirls and decorated
with cutout lime and orange zest petals
and strips of orange and lime zest.

Perfect Cake Coverings

Chapter 3

he covering on a special-occasion cake must
provide a perfect finish and base for the piped,
molded, and/or modeled decorations you will create
to decorate the cake. Two of the most popular
coverings are fondant and royal icing, and there
are specific techniques for applying each of these
to a cake, whether it is round, square, or unusually
shaped. For a super-smooth finish, we advise
adding marzipan to a cake prior to covering it. The
techniques and tips in this chapter will help you
apply marzipan, fondant, and royal icing. With
some practice, your special-occasion cakes will have
a professional touch.

Marzipan

Marzipan is a pliable paste made from ground almonds and a mixture of powdered sugar and egg whites. The exact consistency, texture, and color will vary according to the recipe you use or the type that you buy. Cake decorators use marzipan for modeling, decorating, and covering cakes to keep them moist and to provide smooth, flat surfaces before applying royal icing or fondant.

Homemade marzipan: Homemade marzipan usually has a better flavor than the ready-made variety because you can make it with a higher proportion of ground almonds to sugar. You can also make it in whatever quantity you choose. Take care not to overknead or overhandle marzipan when making it, because this will encourage the oils to flow from the ground almonds, giving an oily covering to a cake that will eventually seep through the icing, causing staining.

Ready-made marzipan: Ready-made marzipan is available in both white and golden forms. Use the white marzipan for all types of cakes; it is the more popular and reliable type, especially for cakes being iced in pastel shades or white. The golden marzipan has added food coloring, and its yellow color may show through thinly applied icing or may cause yellow staining on the surface. Golden marzipan also does not absorb food coloring as well as white marzipan when used for modeling work and decorations.

Marzipan tips: When covering a cake or modeling decorations, always use fresh, pliable marzipan for the best results. To avoid waste, knead the trimmings together and seal them well in a plastic bag for further use. Be sure to allow a marzipanned cake to dry thoroughly before applying the icing; you can do this by storing the cake in a cardboard cake box in a warm, dry room. Properly set marzipan ensures that the cake will hold its shape during icing and prevents any of the cake's moisture from seeping through and staining the surface. Ideally, allow the marzipan to set for twenty-four hours before applying icing (forty-eight hours if using royal icing).

How to Marzipan a Cake for Fondant

When applying marzipan to a cake that will be covered in fondant, smooth the marzipan to the contours of the cake to give it a smooth, rounded finish. This way, the fondant will be free of unsightly lumps and bumps. This is quick and easy to do as long as you ease the marzipan carefully over the sides, corners, and edges of the cake, taking care not to stretch or tear the marzipan at any point. Make sure there are no air bubbles trapped underneath the marzipan on top of the cake before easing the marzipan down the sides.

Round or oval cakes are the simplest shapes to cover because they have only the top and one rounded side to cover smoothly. Square, hexagonal, or other shaped cakes are slightly more difficult to cover with marzipan because of the unusual sides or corners. To prevent the marzipan from stretching or tearing, carefully cup your hands around the base of the corners and gently ease the marzipan up toward the top of the cake. Whatever the shape and size of the cake, the basic method is the same.

Tips for Cakes with Corners

- Gently rub the sides and tops of square and rectangular cakes with your hands or an icing smoother.
- Carefully cup your hands around the base of the cake's corners and gently ease the marzipan up toward the top to prevent stretching or tearing.
- When trimming a cake with a complicated outline, take special care. Work slowly and follow the contours of the cake.

1

2

3

Method for Round Cakes

1. Place the cake on an appropriate cake board and roll the top of the cake carefully with a rolling pin to give it a flat surface. Brush the top and sides of the cake with apricot glaze (see page 205) and dust the work surface lightly with sifted confectioners' sugar.

2. Knead the marzipan into a smooth ball. Roll it out to a ¼-inch (5-mm) thickness in a shape matching that of the cake and large enough to cover the top and sides with about 2–3 inches (5–7½ cm) extra all around. Make sure that the marzipan does not stick to the work surface.

3. Roll the marzipan loosely around the rolling pin and then place the supported marzipan over the cake. Carefully remove it from the rolling pin so that the marzipan falls evenly over the cake. Working from the center of the cake, carefully smooth the marzipan over the top and down the sides, allowing the excess marzipan to spread out on the cake board.

4. Using a sharp knife, cut down onto the board to trim the excess marzipan from the base of the cake.

5. Using clean, dry hands or an icing smoother, gently rub the top of the cake with a circular movement to give a smooth, glossy finish to the marzipan.

6. Leave the marzipanned cake in a warm, dry place for at least two hours, and preferably up to twenty-four hours, before covering it with fondant.

4

5

6

How to Marzipan a Cake for Royal Icing

Marzipanning a cake to prepare it for royal icing is a very exacting process because the underlying shape of the cake is the key to achieving a flat finish with the icing. When covered with marzipan, the cake should look clean, sharp, and smooth.

Achieve the desired result by first marzipanning the top of the cake and then placing the cake on a cake board before applying marzipan to the sides. For a round cake, you can measure and cut one long strip of marzipan to the exact height and circumference of the cake. Square or rectangular cakes need four single pieces for the sides; one piece applied to each side of the cake and cut accurately to ensure square corners.

Once you've covered the cake, smooth together all of the marzipan's seams and joints with an icing spatula and allow the cake to dry in a warm, dry place for forty-eight hours. Dried and set marzipan will ensure that the cake will hold its shape when you apply the royal icing.

Method for Round Cakes

1. Place the cake on an appropriate cake board and roll the top of the cake carefully with a rolling pin to give it a flat surface. Brush the top of the cake with apricot glaze (see page 205). Lightly dust the work surface with confectioners' sugar.

1

2. Knead two-thirds of the marzipan into a ball. Roll it out to a ¼-inch (5-cm) thickness to fit the top of the cake, allowing a little extra all round.

3. Make sure the marzipan is not sticking to the work surface and then invert the cake and place it in the center of the marzipan round. Trim off the excess marzipan to within ½ inch (1 cm) of the cake. Then, using a small, flexible icing spatula, push the marzipan against the side of the cake until the marzipan forms a neat edge all around the cake.

4. Turn the marzipan-topped cake over again and place it in the center of the cake board. Brush the sides with apricot glaze.

5. Measure and cut a piece of string to match the circumference of the cake. Measure and cut another piece of string to match the height of the side of the cake from the board to the top.

6. Roll out the remaining marzipan to a ¼-inch (5 cm) thickness and cut out one side piece to match the length (circumference of cake) and width (height of cake) of the pieces of string.

7. Carefully fit the marzipan strip around the side of the cake and smooth the joint with an icing spatula.

8. Leave the cake in a warm, dry place for forty-eight hours before icing.

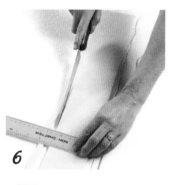

3

6

7

1

2

3

4

5

Method for Square Cakes

1. Place the cake on an appropriate cake board and roll the top of the cake carefully with a rolling pin to flatten the surface. Brush the top with apricot glaze. Lightly dust the work surface with confectioners' sugar.

2. Knead two-thirds of the marzipan into a square shape and roll it out to a ¼-inch (5-mm) thickness to fit the top of the cake, allowing a little extra all around. Invert the cake on the marzipan and trim the excess to within half an inch (1 cm) of the cake's sides. Push the marzipan against the sides with an icing spatula to form a neat edge.

3. Measure the length and height of one side of the cake. Roll out the remaining marzipan and then measure and cut the four side pieces.

4. Brush the sides of the cake with apricot glaze and then carefully fit the pieces to the cake's sides. Smooth all joints with an icing spatula.

5. Leave the marzipanned cake in a warm, dry place for forty-eight hours before icing.

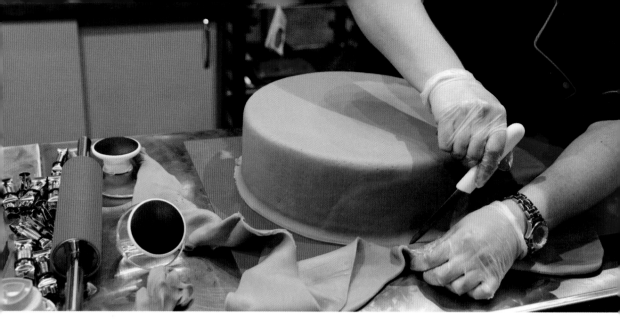

Fondant

Fondant has become popular around the world because of its versatility and ease of use, giving a smooth, softly rounded look to cakes. There are many advantages to using fondant, the most obvious being that it is quick and easy to use. It is soft and pliable and can be rolled out to cover cakes of any shape and size. Even novice cake decorators can achieve a professional finish, and fondant trimmings can be used to make all types of decorations, such as frills, flowers, cutout designs, and modeled animals and figures.

Fondant is easy to make, and there are also ready-made varieties available online or from cake-decorating suppliers. Textures may vary, and some are easier to handle than others, so it is a good idea to try a small quantity before purchasing large amounts of any brand. When you find a brand that you like, buy enough to cover your cake with some extra left over. You will achieve a better finish if you use the same brand for the entire cake rather than mixing and matching varieties. Any extra fondant will keep for several months as long as it's stored in an airtight container.

Fondant is available in white, champagne, pastel and bright colors, and even black. You can color your own fondant, but kneading food coloring into large quantities of fondant is hard, time-consuming work. It also can be quite difficult to obtain an evenly blended color without incorporating some air bubbles into the fondant.

How to Cover Cakes with Fondant

1. Place the marzipanned cake on a cake board of the proper shape and size and set it on a turntable.

2. Dust a work surface with sifted confectioners' sugar to prevent the fondant from sticking. Using more confectioners' sugar if necessary, roll out the fondant to a ¼-inch (5-mm) thickness and in a shape and size to match that of the cake with an overlap generous enough to cover the sides of the cake. Check often to make sure that the fondant is not sticking to the work surface.

3. Brush any excess confectioners' sugar off the fondant and lift it off the work surface, using a rolling pin to support it. Unroll the fondant over the cake to cover it evenly.

4. With hands lightly dusted with cornstarch, smooth the fondant over the top and then down the sides of the cake so the excess fondant is at the base. Be sure to eliminate any air bubbles between the surfaces. If the cake is square, allow the excess fondant to fall over the corners. Then, with cupped hands, smooth the fondant from the base of the corners up to the top to prevent the fondant from tearing or stretching.

5. Smooth the remaining fondant with an icing smoother and then use a small knife to trim off any excess at the base of the cake. Knead the trimmings together and seal them in a plastic bag to use later for decorations.

6. With hands lightly dusted with cornstarch, gently rub the surface of the fondant with a circular movement to give it a smooth and glossy finish.

7. Place the cake in a cake box and leave it in a warm, dry place to allow the fondant to dry.

Covering Cake Boards

There are different ways that you can cover a cake board with fondant to enhance the appearance of the finished cake.

- Cover the whole cake board with fondant, ensuring a smooth, clean finish, and then place the cake in the center of the board.
- Allow enough fondant to cover the cake and the board completely, trimming off the excess around the edge of the board.
- Make and place frills (see page 116) around the base of the cake to cover the board. This can give a very elegant look to a plain fondant cake.
- Trim the joint along the base of the cake with ribbon (see page 99) for a wonderful finishing touch.

Did You Know?

If you're tinting fondant at home, knead food coloring into a small piece of fondant until it is darker than the desired color. Then knead the colored piece into a quantity of white fondant until you've achieved the correct color, the color is even, and the fondant is smooth.

How to Cover Cake Boards with Fondant

1. Brush the cake board with a little apricot glaze (see page 205).
2. Lightly dust a work surface with confectioners' sugar. Roll out the fondant to a ¼-inch (5-mm) thickness in a shape to match the cake board. Make sure that the fondant is not sticking to the work surface.
3. Lift the fondant over the cake board. With hands lightly dusted with cornstarch, or using a cake smoother, smooth the surface of the fondant.
4. Using a small icing spatula, trim the excess fondant. Keep the blade level with the edge of the board and keep the edge of the fondant straight.
5. Leave the covered board in a warm place overnight to dry and then place the iced cake carefully in position on the board.

How to Cover a Cake and Cake Board Together

1. Roll out the fondant so that it is large enough to cover the top and sides of the cake as well as the cake board.

2. Carefully lift the fondant, supported by a rolling pin, over the top of the cake. Unroll the fondant over the cake to cover it evenly.

3. With hands lightly dusted with cornstarch, smooth the fondant over the top and down the sides of the cake and then over the surface of the cake board. Be sure to eliminate any air bubbles between the surfaces.

4. Using an icing spatula, trim off the excess fondant around the edge of the cake board, keeping the blade level with the edge of the board and keeping the edge of the fondant straight.

5. Place the cake and board in a cake box and allow it to dry in a warm, dry place overnight before adding decorations.

Royal Icing

Covering a cake with royal icing is far more time-consuming than covering it with fondant, and it takes patience and practice. However, the end result is a cake with a sparkling finish and classical lines.

To produce a beautifully royal-iced cake, it is essential to start with a well-prepared, level cake that has been carefully marzipanned. You must keep the lines sharp while icing the cake, and you must use royal icing that is light, glossy in texture, and of the correct consistency. With patience, practice, and the right tools, you will achieve great results.

When making royal icing, everything must be spotless. All mixing bowls, sifters, and utensils must be clean and dry, and the working area as dust-free as possible. If possible, wear a white

apron to prevent little bits of clothing lint from getting into the icing; these will come to the surface on a flat coat of icing or even clog a piping tube.

You may use either egg substitute or fresh egg whites to make the icing; both will produce good results. A little lemon juice helps strengthen fresh egg whites, but too much lemon juice will make the icing "short," causing it to break during piping as well as making it difficult to obtain a smooth, flat finish. Do not add glycerin to egg substitute because the icing will not set as hard as fresh egg-white icing.

You must add confectioners' sugar gradually and mix the icing well (rather than beating it each time you add sugar) until you reach the right consistency, which is light and glossy in texture. Alternatively, you may use an electric mixer (especially if you are making a large quantity of royal icing) at the lowest speed until the icing is the correct consistency. Either way, take care not to overmix or aerate the icing. Always allow mixer-made royal icing to stand for twenty-four hours before use and then stir it well to remove any air bubbles.

If you add too much confectioners' sugar too quickly, your royal icing will be heavy and grainy in appearance, rendering it difficult to work with. When set, it will look chalky and dull instead of having a sparkle. It will also be difficult to pipe properly.

Cover royal icing at all times to keep air out and to prevent the surface from drying out and becoming lumpy. Use dampened plastic wrap to seal the surface or place the icing in an airtight container; with the latter, it must be filled to the top with icing to prevent any air from entering the container. Covering the icing with a damp cloth is satisfactory for short periods, but if you leave it overnight, the icing will become diluted from absorbing all of the moisture from the cloth.

Always check the icing regularly during use to make sure that the consistency and texture are correct. If the icing is too stiff, add egg white or egg substitute to make it softer. If the icing is too soft, gradually stir in more sifted confectioners' sugar until you reach the right consistency.

Work from a small quantity of icing in a separate bowl and not from the main batch of royal icing. Be sure to cover the small quantity with damp cheesecloth during use. Keep the icing well scraped down into the bowl so that if the icing becomes dry around the top edges of the bowl, the dryness will not affect the whole batch of icing.

Getting the Right Consistency

The consistency of royal icing is a very important factor because it may affect the result of the icing work. The right consistency for royal icing varies for different uses: a stiff icing that will hold its shape is best for piping; a slightly softer icing that spreads smoothly when a straight edge is pulled across the top is better for flat and peaked icing; and an even looser consistency is required for filling in run-outs (see page 162).

Piping consistency: Stir the icing well with a wooden spoon. When you draw the spoon out of the icing, it should form a fine, sharp point. This consistency, termed *sharp peak*, will flow easily for piping but retain the shape produced by the icing tube used.

Flat- or peaked-icing consistency: Stir the icing well with a wooden spoon. When you draw the spoon out of the icing, it should form a fine point that just curves over at the top. This consistency, termed *soft peak*, spreads smoothly and evenly and creates a flat finish when a straight edge is pulled across the top. You can also pull icing of the same consistency up into soft peaks with an icing spatula to produce peaked icing.

Run-out consistency: Use soft-peak icing to pipe the outlines that will retain the shapes of the run-outs, and then use icing of a thick cream consistency to fill in the shapes. Icing of this consistency will flow to fill in the run-outs but will hold a rounded shape within the piped lines. Make royal icing for run-outs with dried egg whites or egg whites without glycerin so the icing will dry hard and so you can easily remove the run-outs without breakage.

How to Cover a Round Cake Board

1. Once the icing on the cake is completely dry, place the cake and cake board on a turntable and make sure that the cake board is free of any pieces of dry icing. Spread a thin layer of icing evenly around the cake board.
2. Clean up the edge of the board with an icing spatula.
3. Holding the side of the cake board and turntable with one hand, place the icing smoother on the board with the other hand. Turn the cake and turntable for one complete revolution, pulling the straight edge in the opposite direction to smooth the icing. Repeat if the finish is not satisfactory.
4. Using an icing spatula, clean up the edge of the board.
5. Leave the board to dry for at least two hours.
6. Repeat with a second layer of icing to give a smooth finish.

Peaked Royal Icing

Royal icing is very versatile. In addition to being smoothed on a cake to give a perfectly flat finish for decorating, it may be peaked and swirled to give a textured finish. To produce beautifully even peaks, the icing must be of soft-peak consistency. In contrast to applying smooth royal icing, you work on the sides first when making peaks.

First, place a marzipanned cake on a clean cake board. Spread the top and sides of the cake with royal icing to obtain a level surface. Use an icing smoother to level the icing on top of the cake and then use it to smooth the icing on the sides of the cake so that it is fairly even and completely covers the cake.

Give the icing a quick stir and make sure it is the correct soft-peak consistency. Dip one side of the blade of a small, clean icing spatula into the icing. Starting at the base of the cake and working up to the top edge, press the icing onto the iced cake and pull it sharply away to form a peak. Repeat to form three or four peaks in a column up the side of the cake, then dip the icing spatula into the icing again and make another column of peaks down the side of the cake about half an inch (1 cm) over. Stagger the peaks

so they don't align with the adjacent column. Continue in the same manner, making peaks until all sides are completely peaked.

Repeat this process to peak the top of the cake, leaving a smooth area for decorations if desired.

How to Make Royal-Icing Peaks

1. Spread one side of the cake with royal icing and smooth the icing with an icing smoother to obtain a fairly even surface.
2. Press an icing spatula dipped in royal icing on the side of the cake. Pull it away sharply to form a peak. Repeat to form staggered columns of peaks along the side of the cake.

Christmas Tree Cake

Peaked royal icing, with its sparkling texture, is a classic choice for a Christmas cake. This 8-inch (20-cm) rich fruitcake is decorated with a cutout Christmas tree and holly leaves made with special cutters as well as gift-wrapped presents. You can use marzipan or fondant to make these types of decorations (see Chapter 7).

Using Food Coloring

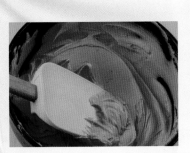

olor is vital to any cake design, whether it is a special-occasion cake decorated with realistic-looking flowers or a festive creation garnished with bright, molded fondant decorations. A comprehensive range of good-quality, concentrated food colorings is available from retailers of cake-decorating supplies. Found as liquids, powders, and pastes, each type has its own use for coloring, tinting, painting, stenciling, and even airbrushing.

Paste and Liquid Coloring

Modern food coloring is very concentrated, so you need to add it in small quantities, whether tinting your icing to a delicate shade or a rich, vibrant color. One method used with liquid food coloring is to dip the end of a toothpick into the color and then add it to the icing. Food coloring does not affect the consistency of marzipan or the various types of icing. Many colors are available, and you can also blend different colors to create desired colors and shades.

It's best to color icings in the daylight and let them dry for at least fifteen minutes before initially assessing the color, because the color of the icings may deepen or lighten upon drying. Because these colors can change quite dramatically when dry, make samples of colored icings and allow them to dry before matching the color of fabric or flowers to the icing.

Types of Food Coloring: 1. Liquid coloring, 2. Dusting brushes, 3. Mixing palette, 4. Luster colors, 5. Petal dusts, 6. Colored fondant decorations, 7. Food-coloring pens, 8. Fondant plaque decorated with food-coloring pens, 9. Paste colorings

At one time, food coloring was available only in liquid form in a range of primary colors. The liquids are still available from most supermarkets and are adequate for tinting icings, frostings, fondant, and marzipan. With careful blending, you can achieve other colors and shades. These colorings, however, are fairly diluted, so they are suitable only for quite light colors; you would need several spoonfuls of this type of food coloring to create strong, rich colors, and that much food coloring would dilute the consistency of what you are trying to color.

How to Color Buttercream Frosting

Buttercream frosting will take more food coloring because fat-based frostings do not color as readily as sugar-based frostings.

1. Add the food coloring to the frosting using a toothpick dipped in the food coloring.
2. Beat the frosting to blend the food coloring evenly throughout the mixture.
3. Add more food coloring with a toothpick if the color is not deep enough.

How to Color Royal Icing

Royal icing will take color very quickly, so take care to add the coloring drop by drop.

1. Add a drop of food coloring on the tip of a toothpick to the icing.
2. Mix the food coloring into the royal icing with a wooden spoon until the icing is evenly colored.
3. Add more food coloring, one drop at a time, if necessary.

1

2

How to Color Marzipan

Because it contains ground almonds, marzipan is oil based and thus will need more food coloring to obtain deeper shades of color.

1. Add the food coloring to the marzipan using a toothpick dipped in the color.
2. Knead the marzipan until the color is evenly distributed.
3. Add more food coloring if needed to obtain the desired color.

Bunny Big Ears

This brightly colored cake makes a great young person's birthday cake. Use buttercream to frost an 8-inch (20-cm) square cake and pipe the edges with swirls. Top each swirl with alternating beads of black, green, and red fondant. Roll out a piece of white fondant and cover it with alternating strips of black, green, and red fondant. Cut out the shape with a cookie cutter.

How to Paint Sugar Pieces

1. Make sure the fondant pieces are dry. Using a fine paintbrush and food coloring gel, paint each piece until evenly colored.
2. Using a fine paintbrush and liquid food coloring, paint the oak leaves slightly unevenly to give a more realistic finish.
3. Arrange the dry colored sugar pieces as a border pattern to decorate an 8-inch (20 cm) round cake covered with fondant.

Collage Cake

This design is made from two basic fondant shapes painted with bright gel colors to create an interesting pattern. Match the ribbons to the cutout sugar pieces.

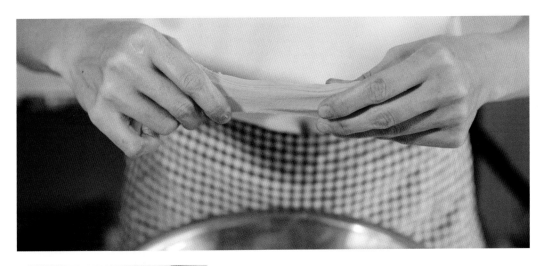

How to Color Fondant

Fondant colors easily, so take care to add the food coloring just a little at a time.

1. Add a drop of food coloring to the fondant with a toothpick.
2. Knead the icing with your fingertips to incorporate the food coloring evenly throughout the icing.
3. Add more color, a drop at a time, and knead if required to reach the correct shade.

Evenly colored buttercream icing, royal icing, marzipan, and fondant, ready to use.

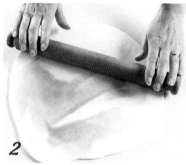

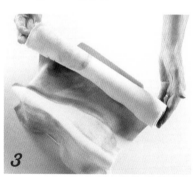

How to Marble Fondant with One Color

1. Dip a toothpick into food coloring paste and insert the toothpick into the fondant so that the color penetrates into the center. Repeat to insert the color about eight times.
2. Turn the ball of fondant over so the colored marks are underneath. Roll out the fondant thin, revealing the marbled design.
3. Support the fondant over a rolling pin and unroll it over the cake to cover evenly.
4. Using lightly cornstarched palms, smooth the fondant evenly over the cake to obtain an even finish.

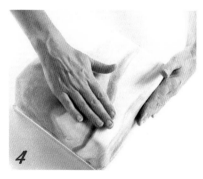

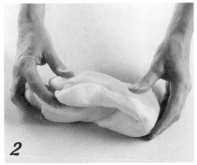

How to Marble Fondant with Three Colors

1. Roll each of three different-colored pieces of fondant into a sausage shape and then cut each piece in half.
2. Press the pieces of fondant together in alternating order and roll into one long sausage shape. Fold the sausage shape in three.
3. Roll out the fondant thinly enough to cover the cake.
4. Support the fondant over a rolling pin and unroll it over the cake to cover evenly.
5. Using lightly cornstarched palms, smooth the fondant evenly over the cake to obtain an even finish.

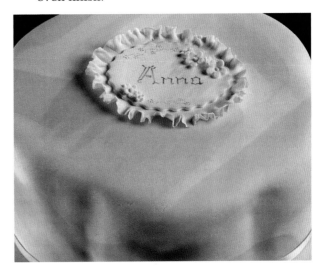

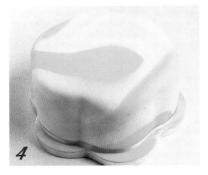

Marbled Cake

A petal-shaped cake covered with tricolor-marbled fondant makes a bright birthday or special-occasion cake. The frilled plaque is made from fondant decorated with flower blossoms from a plunger cutter, and the name is written with a food-coloring pen. The edges of the plaque were brushed with petal dust.

Petal Dusts

These powdered colors can be brushed or "dusted" onto molded and cutout flowers, sugar pieces, and molded decorations; you can even apply them to cake surfaces. You apply petal dusts when the icing is absolutely dry, which is particularly useful for last-minute work; for example, if matching colors to fresh flowers in season. Applying the dust to dry icing allows you to add a touch of color to the finished item without the risk of color running into the icing, which may happen when you use paste colors.

Available in a wide range of colors, petal dusts are especially suitable for blending, either in a palette or by applying different colors on top of the other. Petal dusts hold their color without fading. They are more expensive than liquid or gel food coloring, but they are well worth having because they last for so long.

How to Dust with Petal Dusts

1. Choose the powdered colors required to color the flowers on your cake and place a little of each color on an icing palette.
2. Using a dusting brush, brush the dry sugar flowers, blending the colors to give an attractive, realistic effect.

Springtime Cake

An oval cake topped with delicate cutout fondant flowers and leaves that were cut out using various cutters and dried completely before coloring, is perfect for a springtime celebration. The flowers are tinted with a blend of differently colored petal dusts and luster dusts, and the leaves are painted unevenly with green liquid food coloring for a realistic finish.

Luster Dusts

Luster dusts are meant for specialized work and are available in gold, silver, and a range of colors. All colors contain sparkle or glitter that gives a metallic sheen, making them especially popular for festive occasions. Luster dusts come in powdered form and need to be mixed with a clear alcohol, such as gin or vodka, before being applied to the dried fondant or icing according to the manufacturer's instructions. You also must ensure that you use nontoxic, edible versions of these products. Note that there are some varieties labeled as nontoxic but are not intended for consumption.

Summer Cake

This strawberry design is hand-painted on a fondant plaque, and the wild strawberries and leaves are made from fondant. This design looks bright on the crisp, clean lines of the royal-iced cake. Write a name or message in the center of the plaque for a special person or occasion.

Food-Coloring Pens

These pens look like felt-tip pens but are filled with edible food coloring. They come in a range of colors and have innumerable uses, especially for quick decorating, writing, and applying details to models or sugar pieces. Simply use them as you would a pen to write a name or message, to draw designs on dry royal-icing run-outs or small sugar plaques, or even to make a design directly on an iced cake. Food-coloring pens are must-haves for your collection of cake-decorating tools.

How to Use Food-Coloring Pens

1. On a dry fondant plaque, use a black food-coloring pen to draw the freehand design.
2. Using red and green food-coloring pens, color the strawberries and strawberry stems and leaves.
3. Color the last leaf to complete the whole design.

1

2

3

Autumn Cake

The fondant plaque is made separately
and the design is completed with food-
coloring pens. Once the fondant is dry,
lightly draw the freehand design on the
cake with a black food-coloring pen
and then color in the details.

Instant Decorations

How to Make a Fresh Flower Spray

1. Wrap the stem of each fresh flower with 4 inches (10 cm) of floral wire.
2. Bind the wire and stem of each flower with floral tape.
3. Gather the flowers together and arrange them into a spray. Tape the flowers together, one at a time, working down the stems until all of the flowers are secured.
4. Carefully bend the wires to create a shape that will sit neatly on top of the cake.

Shamrock Cake

This unusual shamrock-shaped cake is covered in fondant and trimmed with ribbon and displays a fresh flower arrangement in complementary colors.

Silk Flowers

Artificial flowers can look very real and are available from cake-decorating retailers, craft stores, and florists. They come in a wide range of blooms and sprays and can serve as instant, reusable decorations on many types of cakes.

How to Make a Silk Flower Arrangement

1. Cut off each bloom from the silk sprays and wire them separately onto 4-inch (10-cm) lengths of floral wire.
2. Cover the wire on each flower's stem with floral tape.
3. Arrange the flowers together to form your chosen spray and then tape them securely together with floral tape.
4. Add ribbon tails to finish the silk flower arrangement.

Sugar-Frosted Flowers

These delicate decorations are simply fresh flowers preserved with a mixture of egg white and sugar. Once completely dry, they will last for several weeks. You can pair them with colorful ribbons tied into pretty bows, loops, and tails, and you may also wire them and fashion them into sprays before frosting. After frosting, either use the flowers immediately or store them carefully between sheets of tissue paper in a box in a warm, dry place until you need to use them.

Choose simple small flowers with fairly flat petals, such as violets, primroses, tiny daffodils or freesia, and firm herb or fruit leaves. Choose young blooms, and pick or buy the flowers and leaves just before you need to frost them.

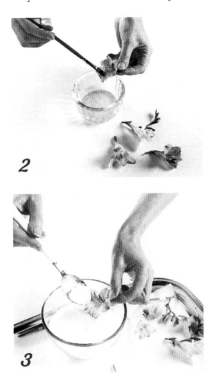

2

3

How to Make Sugar-Frosted Flowers

1. Dry the flowers and leaves with paper towels, if necessary, and try to leave a small stem intact on each bloom. Place some superfine granulated sugar on a plate or in a bowl.
2. Using a fine paintbrush, paint both sides of the flower petals, leaves, and stems with lightly beaten egg white.
3. Spoon the sugar over the petals, leaves, and stems to coat them evenly on both sides.
4. Carefully shake the flowers to remove any excess sugar and gently arrange the coated petals and leaves on a wire rack covered with paper towels.
5. Store the flowers in a warm, dry place until dry. Position them in a way that will help keep their shape; some flowers and leaves dry better with their stems upward and their petals or leaves flat on the paper.

Sugar-Frosted Flower Cake

This delicate 8-inch (20-cm) cake is covered with marzipan and fondant. The edge is crimped, and the cake and board are trimmed with mauve ribbons and sugar-frosted freesia and minute orchids chosen to match the fondant and ribbons.

How to Make Sugar-Frosted Fruit

You can frost fruit in the same way as flowers. Choose small, fresh fruit such as grapes, cherries, strawberries and other berries, lychees, or kumquats in peak condition.

1. Wipe the fruit so that all surfaces are completely dry.
2. Brush each piece of fruit evenly with lightly beaten egg white.
3. Carefully spoon superfine granulated sugar over the fruit to cover it evenly.
4. Allow the fruit to dry on paper towels in a warm, dry place.

2

3

Using Ribbons

Ribbons are a nonedible type of decoration that is guaranteed to transform even the simplest cakes into something quite special. There are many types of ribbon to choose from in different widths, colors, and textures, as well as with plain or fancy edges, that are suitable for all types of cakes.

The most popular ribbon for decoration is double-faced polyester satin, which you can use to make bows, loops, and tails for cakes and flower sprays. You can also use it to band cake boards and to fit around the sides of cakes to match their designs and colors.

Trimming Cake Boards

To trim a cake board, choose a ribbon the same width as the edge of the cake board in a color to contrast with or complement an element of the finished cake. An additional option is to pin a narrow band of contrasting ribbon on top of the first ribbon, using stainless-steel pins.

Ribbon Pictures

You can use ribbons to make simple designs or pictures to decorate the top of a cake. Plan the design on paper first and then simply cut the ribbons to size and apply them to the cake by painting the ends with royal icing to affix them to the cake's surface. Use ribbons of different textures, widths, and colors.

Did You Know?

Always remember to remove inedible decorations from the cake before cutting.

1

How to Make a Ribbon Picture

1. Cut the various ribbons to length and place them roughly in position, moving the pieces and changing the colors until you are pleased with the design.
2. Secure all ribbon pieces to the cake's surface with royal icing. This ribbon picture has been applied to a fondant plaque instead of directly to the top of the cake so it can be removed and kept as a memento.

Bows, Loops, and Tails

Attach neat, tiny bows to the sides or top of a cake. You can team them with wider ribbons around the cake to produce a quick yet elegant decoration. Tiny ribbon bows add delicate touches to a cake's design and they can be made in various colors and sizes, using different widths of ribbon. Tie the bows neatly—tweezers are sometimes useful for minuscule ones—and you can either trim off the tails or curl the tails by pulling the ends over a scissor blade.

2

Ribbon loops look pretty in sprays of flowers or arranged with molded sugar flowers. You can wire several shades of ribbon loops with curled tail ends

1

together and arrange them on the cake with sugar-frosted, silk, or sugar flowers.

For loop designs ranging from simple to flamboyant, fold the ribbon into single, double, or triple (or more) loops using one or several colors. Secure the loops with floral wire and finish with floral tape if needed (1 and 2).

Loop or fold ribbons into a variety of shapes to make decorative ribbon tails (3 and 4). Secure the loops into position on the cake with beads of royal icing.

2

3

4

Ribbon Picture Cake

This 8-inch (20-cm) cake is covered with marzipan and fondant and displays a fondant plaque simply decorated with ribbons cut to make a flowerpot full of flowers.

Decorating
with Chocolate

hocolate comes in many forms: as milk,
semisweet, dark, and white chocolate bars
and chips; as thick, richly flavored spreads; as
unsweetened cocoa powder or drinking chocolate;
and even distilled into smooth liqueurs. Be sure to
choose the right chocolate for what you are making
and follow the manufacturer's guidelines to obtain
the best results.

Choosing Chocolate

Selecting the right type of chocolate for cake decoration can be quite daunting because there are so many varieties and flavors from which to choose. The ingredient that determines the quality of the chocolate is the cocoa butter, which is very expensive. The more cocoa butter in the chocolate, the finer the texture and the richer the flavor. The original cocoa butter found in chocolate is often replaced with different percentages of vegetable fat, separating chocolate into different levels of quality for a variety of uses.

The darker the chocolate, the harder the texture and the stronger the flavor. Milk chocolate is mild and sweet, while white chocolate is sweet with no distinctive chocolate flavor. Here's a more detailed look at different types of chocolate.

Couverture: This the finest and most expensive kind of chocolate, made entirely with cocoa butter, which produces a chocolate of superior quality, flavor, and texture. It is available from specialty retailers and must be tempered before use.

Tempering chocolate is a very exacting process. Cocoa butter is an unstable substance made of a number of individual fats that all melt at different

Did You Know?

White chocolate lends itself to being colored, especially for decorating or coating. Use oil-based or powdered food coloring because any liquids added to chocolate will cause it to thicken and render it unusable.

temperatures. To successfully temper couverture chocolate, you have to carefully heat it and cool it to different temperatures, so beginners are advised to leave this task to more experienced hands.

Baking chocolate: This is a good, all-around chocolate suitable for all types of recipes. The quality depends on how much cocoa butter has been retained, which also affects the flavor, color, and texture of the chocolate. Baking chocolate comes in different varieties, such as unsweetened, semisweet, and bittersweet. It is easy to work with and melts readily to a consistency suitable for spreading, coating, dipping, and piping.

Dessert or eating chocolate: This type of chocolate has a wonderful flavor and refined texture. It is more expensive than cooking chocolate, so if you plan to bake with it, save it for special desserts, chocolate candies, or chocolate decorations.

Chocolate-flavored cake covering: This type of chocolate is widely available, easy to use, and less expensive to buy. It is called *chocolate-flavored* instead of *chocolate* because it has more vegetable fat than cocoa butter, giving it a poorer flavor as well as a rather soft and greasy texture. When melted, it gets very liquid and sets quickly. Being soft, it is ideal for quick chocolate curls shaved directly from the block. You may use it in any recipe that calls for chocolate, but remember that the flavor is not going to be as good as that of real chocolate.

Types of Chocolate: 1. Milk chocolate couverture, 2. Semisweet cake covering, 3. Milk chocolate cake covering, 4. Luxury semisweet baking chocolate, 5. Cocoa powder, 6. Semisweet baking chocolate, 7. White chocolate chips, 8. White dessert chocolate, 9. Semisweet dessert chocolate, 10. Luxury semisweet baking chocolate, 11. Semisweet chocolate chips, 12. Milk chocolate chips, 13. White cake covering, 14. Milk chocolate cake covering

Melting Chocolate

Melting chocolate is a precise task if you want the chocolate to set to a smooth, glossy appearance. For dipping chocolates, cookie coatings, or cut-out chocolate pieces and decorations, use the following guidelines:

- Always use fresh chocolate to ensure a good flavor.
- Never allow moisture, steam, or condensation to come into contact with chocolate or it will become thick and unstable.
- Leave the bowl over the hot water during use unless you want the chocolate to thicken.
- For speed, use a microwave to melt the chocolate. Start by checking that there is no previous condensation in the microwave because it will affect the chocolate when melted. Place the chocolate pieces in a microwave-safe bowl and heat on the lowest

White Chocolate Cake

This 8-inch (20-cm) chocolate sandwich cake was covered with a smooth layer of buttercream frosting before being coated with melted white chocolate. The top edge is decorated with a shell edging of chocolate and hazelnut spread, and the top and sides are finished with chocolate cutout pieces.

setting for three or four minutes, until the chocolate has almost melted, and then stir until smooth.

• If you overheat the chocolate during the melting process, it will not be ideal for covering a cake, but you can still use it as an ingredient in cakes, desserts, and other recipes that call for melted chocolate.

• Store any leftover melted chocolate to use at a later date. Wrap it in foil to keep air out and store it for up to one month in a cool, dry place.

How to Melt Chocolate

1. Break the chocolate into small pieces and place them in a large, clean, dry bowl over a saucepan of hot water. Make sure the base of the bowl does not touch the water, and do not heat the water further.

2. Stir the chocolate when it has melted completely, making sure to never exceed 100–110°F (38–43°C).

Using Melted Chocolate as a Coating

1

2

Melted chocolate can be used to coat all types of edible items—from entire cakes to individual pieces of candy and fruit—completely or partially with a delicious glossy covering. It's easy to dip small items into a bowl of melted chocolate with a confectioners' dipping fork or other large fork and then set them on parchment paper to dry.

How to Dip Candy

1. Dip the candy pieces, one at a time, into a bowl of melted chocolate using a dipping fork or other large fork.
2. Remove and tap the fork to allow the excess chocolate to fall.
3. Place the dipped candy pieces on parchment paper to set.

1

3

4

How to Coat a Cake with Chocolate

1. Melt the chocolate in a bowl and check the consistency. Wipe the condensation from the outside of the bowl.
2. Place the cake on a wire cooling rack over parchment paper.
3. In one movement, tip the bowl of chocolate over the cake so that the chocolate flows over the top and evenly down the sides.
4. Shake the wire rack gently to encourage the chocolate to flow.

Chocolate-Covered Cake with Fresh Fruit

Two 8-inch (20-cm) cakes, one chocolate and one vanilla, are each split into two layers. Alternate layers are sandwiched together and covered with whipped dairy cream flavored with melted chocolate. The cake is then completely coated in melted semisweet chocolate to give a luxurious glossy finish and decorated with chocolate-dipped fresh fruit and chocolate leaves.

1 *2* *4*

How to Dip Fruit

1. Make sure the fruit is dry and at room temperature.
2. Hold the stalk end of the fruit and carefully dip the fruit into the melted chocolate.
3. Gently shake the fruit to allow the excess chocolate to fall.
4. Leave the dipped pieces of fruit to set on baking parchment.

A selection of colorful fruits, half-dipped in either semisweet, milk, or white chocolate, looks very appealing.

Did You Know?

Always ensure that anything you want to coat with or dip into chocolate is at room temperature or the chocolate will set before coating smoothly.

How to Make Chocolate Leaves

1. Choose small, firm leaves with well-defined veins from flowers, herbs, or other types of plants. Use the leaves when they are still fresh and dry them thoroughly with paper towels.
2. Using a medium-size paintbrush, thickly coat the underside of each leaf with melted chocolate. Do not paint over its edge, or the leaf will not peel away from the chocolate.
3. Place the leaves on parchment paper, chocolate side up, in a cool place to set.
4. Just before using the chocolate leaves as decorations, peel the real leaves away from the chocolate and discard.

2 *3* *4*

Piping with Chocolate

Melted chocolate is quite difficult to pipe through a metal tube because the coldness of the metal sets the chocolate before it can be piped. One way around this is to add a few drops of glycerin to the chocolate to thicken it (rather than allow the chocolate to cool and thicken) and then pipe it through a tube as quickly as possible. If the chocolate does start to set, warm the piping tube in your hands. If you only need to pipe simple decorative threads or chocolate outlines (for piped chocolate pieces and chocolate run-outs, for example), use a parchment-paper piping bag with the end snipped off to a point. The simplest solution of all is to use chocolate hazelnut spread because it has the ideal consistency.

Always choose simple shapes for offset piping: stylized flowers work well for piped pieces, and animals, hearts, flowers, bells, horseshoes, numbers, or letters are ideal choices for run-outs. Cookie cutters make excellent templates for these types of designs.

Using Chocolate Spread
Fit a parchment-paper piping bag with a small star tube, fill the bag with chocolate hazelnut spread, and use it to pipe attractive borders.

1

3

How to Pipe Chocolate Pieces

1. Draw the chosen designs on a piece of paper. Place parchment paper on top of your drawing paper and secure the corners in place with tape.
2. Fill a parchment-paper piping bag with melted chocolate, fold down the top, and snip off the end.
3. Pipe fine threads of chocolate, following the outlines of your designs, or pipe freehand designs.
4. Allow the chocolate to set and then carefully slide a thin icing spatula under each piece to loosen it from the paper and use for decorating.

Did You Know?

For simple chocolate lines and threads, take a parchment-paper piping bag and snip off the end to make whatever size hole you need.

Feathered Cake

This 8-inch (20-cm) chocolate cake was baked in a springform pan and then split into three layers, filled and covered with whipped cream, and coated with melted semisweet chocolate and feathered with white chocolate. The top is piped with whipped-cream stars and decorated with piped chocolate pieces.

How to Make Chocolate Run-Outs

1. Draw or trace the chosen shape several times—to allow for breakages—on a piece of paper. Place a piece of parchment paper over the top and secure the edges in place with tape.

2. Using two parchment-paper piping bags, half-fill each with melted chocolate and fold down the tops. Snip off the point from one piping bag and pipe a thread of chocolate around the edge of the design. You may achieve better results if you wait for the chocolate to thicken slightly because you will then obtain a clean thread of chocolate.

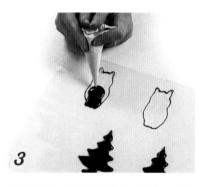

3. Cut the end off the remaining piping bag and fill in the run-out with melted chocolate so that it looks rounded and over-filled. Leave to set completely.

4. Pipe in any details or designs, if necessary, and then allow to harden. Carefully peel off the paper and use the run-outs as decorations. You can prepare these run-outs in advance and store them for later use.

here are many uses for fondant besides simply covering cakes. You can cut out, mold, frill, crimp, and emboss this pliable paste and use it in many other exciting ways. Marzipan is also smooth, soft, and easy to work with; it can be cut into shapes or molded into flowers and animal figures. Both mediums may be tinted and colored with food coloring, making them ideal for decorative work.

Crimping and Embossing

There are two very useful techniques that provide a quick way to decorate cakes covered in fondant or marzipan: crimping and embossing.

To crimp the covered surface of a cake, you literally pinch the fondant or marzipan with crimpers, a tool that looks like large tweezers. Crimping around the top edge of a cake is a popular technique, but you can also crimp around the base, on the sides, or across the top. Crimpers are available with differently shaped and sized end pieces, producing curved lines, scallops, ovals, V shapes, hearts, diamonds, zigzags, and more.

To polish your technique and to obtain an even crimped design, practice on a spare piece of fondant or marzipan before working on a cake. Always crimp on a freshly covered cake.

How to Crimp a Design

1. Start with a clean crimper and dust it with cornstarch to prevent sticking.
2. Place the crimper on the edge of the cake and squeeze firmly to mark the fondant or marzipan. Gently release and lift off the crimper; if it springs apart, it will tear the fondant or marzipan. Place the crimper next to the marked pattern and repeat the process. Continue crimping all around the top of the cake, occasionally dipping the crimper in cornstarch.

Embossing tools stamp a design on the cake's surface, and they are available in a spectrum of patterns and designs. Regular household items— such as spoon handles, tops of icing tubes, or anything small with a defined outline—will also work to impress a pattern into the fondant.

You can add color to an embossed design by painting part or all of the design with a fine brush and food coloring, brushing the design with petal dusts, or drawing with food-coloring pens. Dipping the embossing tool into colored petal dust before embossing will imprint the pattern with the color. Practice all of these techniques on a remnant of fondant or marzipan before trying them on a freshly covered cake.

How to Emboss a Pattern

1. Dust the embossing tool with cornstarch (or petal dust, if you want color).
2. Press the embossing tool into the fondant to the same depth and at the same angle each time.
3. Dust with cornstarch or petal dust and continue around the cake until the design is complete.

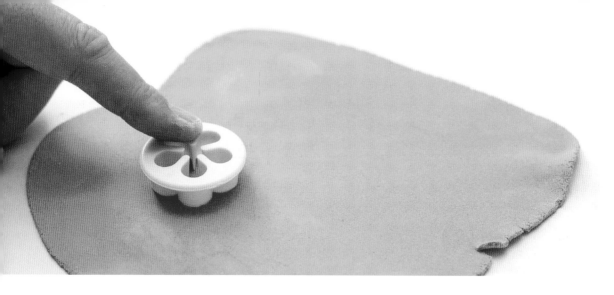

Making Cut-Out Decorations

There are many types of cutters to make cut-out decorations from marzipan and fondant, including cookie cutters, hors d'oeuvre cutters, frill cutters, and specialized flower and leaf cutters. Alternatively, you can use homemade card-stock templates to cut out your own designs. Following a few basic techniques, it is a simple method of making attractive decorations. The skill comes in applying the pieces to the cake's surface, but the results are well worth the effort.

Simple cutouts make instant decorations for any iced cake. Prepare your work surface by lightly dusting it with sifted confectioner's sugar and then roll out your fondant to a thickness of about ⅛ of an inch (3 mm). Use your chosen cutters to cut out shapes.

Always allow fondant cutouts to dry before applying them to the cake's surface with egg white or royal icing. Alternatively—especially if you need a lot of cut-out pieces to decorate a large cake or several tiers—you can make them in advance and store them in a box in a warm, dry place until you are ready to use them. With marzipan cutouts, you should apply them directly to the cake and secure them in place with apricot glaze (see page 205).

Did You Know?

If you are coloring your fondant before making cut-out decorations, make sure that the color is evenly distributed before you roll the fondant out.

Use the cutouts to form an attractive border or side decoration. Make a flower design for the top of a cake using small flower and leaf cutters, cutting stems from thin strips, and marking the leaves' veins with a knife. You can dry leaf cutouts curved over a dowel for a three-dimensional effect.

For a truly individual cut-out decoration, use a picture or pattern as inspiration (think greeting cards and wallpaper designs) and make templates as a guide. Cut out the individual components of the picture from colored marzipan or fondant and assemble them on the cake. Once you've re-created the picture or design, secure each piece and add detail with food-coloring pens.

How to Make Cutouts

1. Roll the fondant or marzipan thinly. Use a variety of cutters to cut out as many shapes as you need to complete the design.
2. Arrange the shapes to form a border, side decoration, or top design, securing fondant pieces with royal icing and marzipan pieces with apricot glaze.

Christening Cake

An 8-inch (20-cm) oval cake covered with marzipan and fondant makes a pretty christening cake. The cut-out fondant hearts and blossoms are easy to make with plunger cutters. The bib is made from gum paste and may be removed from the cake and kept as a memento.

Doily Cake
Cut-out filigree sugar pieces, attached to the base and top of this cake, give the effect of a doily design. Cut-out pieces from a plunger heart cutter were used on the top and side of the cake. This sharp, clear design enhances the precise lines of a royal-iced cake, and the cake may be personalized with a name in the center.

Making Sugar Pieces and Extensions

You can make delicate pieces out of fondant and allow them to dry for several days. However, extension pieces are best made from gum paste (see Chapter 9) because they dry quickly, and they need to be fine yet strong because they are usually attached to the edges of the cake to extend the design. You can create many wonderful shapes from fondant or gum paste using cutters, icing-tube tips, and crimpers. Figure out the design first and then make a few test pieces to try on the iced cake so you can calculate how many pieces you'll need. You can color the fondant or paste if needed, or you can dust the pieces with petal dust when they are dry.

How to Make Sugar Pieces and Extensions

1. Roll out the fondant or gum paste in small quantities (gum paste dries particularly quickly). Roll it so thinly that you can almost see through it. Using cutters of varying shapes and sizes, or a template, cut out as many pieces from the rolled-out paste as you can.

2. Arrange the pieces on a flat surface dusted with cornstarch and leave them in a warm, dry place until hard. Repeat this process if you need to make more extensions or sugar pieces to decorate the cake.

3. When the pieces are dry, brush them with petal dust, if desired, and arrange them roughly on the cake to ensure the design fits properly.

4. Attach the sugar pieces to the cake with royal icing and allow them to dry overnight in a covered box in a warm, dry place.

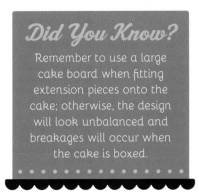

Did You Know?

Remember to use a large cake board when fitting extension pieces onto the cake; otherwise, the design will look unbalanced and breakages will occur when the cake is boxed.

Appliqué Cake

This simple floral design, taken from an upholstery pattern, has been transformed into a stunning fondant design on a round white cake that is suitable for many occasions, especially for someone who appreciates flowers. Use any 8-inch (20-cm) fondant-covered cake as a base for the design.

Decorating with Appliqué Designs

This is a very clever way of decorating a plain iced cake with a cut-out fondant or marzipan design that covers the top and sides of the cake. Inspiration for appliqué designs often comes from fabric patterns, wallpaper prints, or embroidery designs.

Once you've covered your cake in fondant and chosen a design, trace the detail of the design accurately onto parchment paper to make a complete template. Select the color(s) for the chosen design and tint the fondant or marzipan accordingly. Alternatively, leave the fondant or marzipan in its original color and paint it with food coloring after you've cut out the design.

Dust the work surface with confectioner's sugar and roll out the fondant or marzipan thinly. Using a small, sharp knife, cut out the design pieces and apply them one by one to the cake, taking care not to overhandle or distort the pieces. Press them gently into position to form the design.

Another method is to knead equal parts of gum paste and fondant together so the fondant design sets hard before you apply it to the cake. The advantage of this method is that the pieces may be applied so that they stand off from the cake or can be set at an angle while still holding their shape to give a three-dimensional appearance to the decorations.

How to Make Appliqué Designs

1. Trace the design on a piece of parchment paper.
2. Roll out the colored fondant thinly, place the pattern on top of the fondant, and mark the design with a pin or marker.
3. Cut out the design on the fondant with a sharp knife.
4. Arrange the cut-out pieces on the paper design to ensure they fit before securing them to the cake.
5. Place the sugar pieces carefully in position on the cake and attach them with a little egg white or royal icing.

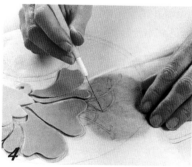

Wedgwood Cake

This cake's hexagonal shape lends itself to scalloped fondant frills finished with a crimped edge and decorated with a tiny cut-out fondant heart border. The top is decorated with a small arrangement of silk flowers held together with ribbon. The 10-inch (25-cm) cake is covered with marzipan and blue fondant with a tiny shell border piped from a writing tube before the frills were applied.

Making Advanced Fondant Decorations

The following decorating techniques—frills and flounces, ribbon insertion, and eyelet lace (*broderie anglaise*)—will require a little more time and patience to master. However, the finished effects are quite stunning and will be the focal point of any special-occasion cake.

The following instructions will lead you carefully through the steps of each method, but you should practice the techniques on dummy cakes or using fondant trimmings until you are completely satisfied with the results and feel ready to attempt the real thing.

Did You Know?

To make colored frills, either tint the fondant beforehand or brush the dried frills with petal dust; the latter will achieve a softer effect.

Let your fondant-covered cake dry overnight before applying fondant frills so you do not mark the cake while you're applying the frills.

Frills and Flounces

Frills and flounces look spectacular when attached to a cake of any shape, whether in single layers, in several layers, in scalloped or arched designs, or simply attached to the base of the cake to cover the cake board. Their appearance may be further enhanced by crimping the edge of the frill where it is attached to the cake, piping details above and below the frills, embossing the top edges of the frills, or incorporating ribbon-insertion designs.

1

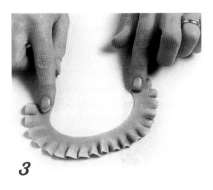

2

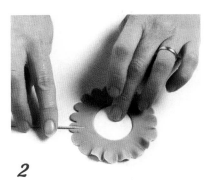

3

It is easy to make fondant frills; however, frills made of fondant have a tendency to drop if they are applied too quickly. It is recommended to knead one part gum paste (see Chapter 9) into two parts fondant so the frills set more quickly.

How to Make Frills

1. On a surface lightly dusted with cornstarch, roll out a small piece of fondant thinly and evenly until you can almost see through it. Cut out a 3-inch (7½-cm) round using a fluted cutter. Then, using a 1½-inch (4-cm) plain round cutter, cut out and remove the center of the round. Alternatively, you can use a garrett cutter, which is especially made for cutting out frills. Make sure the fondant is not sticking to the work surface.

2. Place the end of a toothpick sprinkled with cornstarch on the outer edge of the circle. Roll the toothpick backward and forward along the edge of each flute with your fingers until the edge of the fondant begins to frill. Continue this process around the entire edge of the fondant circle until the edge is completely frilled.

3. Cut the ring open with a sharp knife and then gently ease the frill open. Turn the frill over so the neat side shows.

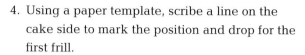

4. Using a paper template, scribe a line on the cake side to mark the position and drop for the first frill.
5. Pipe a line of royal icing following the line where you will attach the frill.
6. Press the frill gently in position. Trim if necessary to achieve a perfect fit.
7. Lift the base of the frill slightly with a plastic modeling tool, if necessary, so it stands away from the cake side.
8. Repeat this procedure to attach more frills around the cake. If you wish, add extra layers above the frills already attached to make a multi-frilled design. Finish the top edge of the frill with a crimper or embossing tool.
9. Inverted frills are an attractive alternative, giving a "ruffled" appearance. The method for making and applying them is the same.

Peach Wedding Cake

Softly frilled champagne fondant is the main feature of the top tier of this simple but beautiful cake decorated with peach-colored flowers made with a blossom plunger cutter, ribbons, and bows. The fresh flower arrangement beautifully complements the delicate coloring of the ribbons and fondant.

How to Make a Frilled Plaque

1. Roll out fondant thinly on a surface dusted with cornstarch.
2. Cut out the plaque using a fluted cutter in the desired shape and size.
3. Frill the edge using a toothpick as previously described and then allow the plaque to dry on a flat surface.
4. Dust the plaque with petal dust to color (optional) and pipe with royal icing to decorate. Alternatively, use food-coloring pens to write on the plaque and add the design or border.

Ribbon Insertion

This technique creates the effect of threading a single piece of ribbon through the fondant. The design can be straight, diagonal, or curved and combined with crimper work or dainty piping to make it an even more special feature.

It is important to plan the design accurately, using a template to make the insertions into the fondant, because it is very noticeable if the ribbon insertions are uneven. First, choose a ribbon in a color and width that will complement the shape and design of the cake. Then, plan the design on paper. Cut as many pieces of ribbon as you need, making sure that the

ribbon pieces are slightly longer than the space between insertion points so that you have enough excess to tuck both ends into the icing. When you are ready to transfer the design onto your cake, the cake should be freshly covered with fondant and firm on the surface but soft underneath.

How to Insert Ribbons

1. Using a stainless-steel pin or scribing tool, mark the design accurately on a freshly fondant-covered cake. Using a very fine blade, cut the slits accurately in the icing following the lines you just marked.
2. Carefully insert one end of a piece of ribbon into a slit, using a pin or fine blade.
3. Tuck the other end of the ribbon into the next slit in the same way and press gently in place.
4. Leave a space and repeat the ribbon-insertion steps with the other pieces of ribbon until all the slits are filled.
5. Finish off the ribbon insertion with tiny bows, fine piping, or crimping.

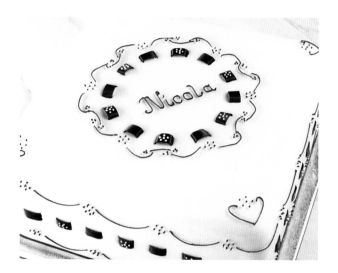

Eyelet Lace

The dainty design of eyelet lace can be applied directly to a fondant-covered cake or made in the shape of a sugar plaque and placed on the cake. It looks just like a piece of embroidery; in fact, you'll find inspiration for this type of cake decoration from paper embroidery patterns, table linens, fabric prints, and porcelain designs. Traditional eyelet lace has a scalloped edge that is finished with a buttonhole stitch or petit point. This can be interpreted on a cake using a #0 piping tube and royal icing, marking out the pattern using a knitting needle.

To make a round template, measure out, on a piece of paper, the size of the plaque to fit the cake; it should be about 1 inch (2½ cm) smaller than the top of the cake. Cut out the paper plaque template. Draw and mark the design accurately on the paper template and then cut out the scalloped edge by folding the round paper template in half several times to form a narrow cone shape, drawing a semicircle at the broad end of the cone, and cutting around the semicircle to make the scallops. Open up the template and press it flat before placing it on the fondant.

Eyelet Lace Cake

The delicate design of this eyelet lace plaque was marked out and piped before the plaque was applied to the cake. The center design is transferred to the sides of the cake and piped in contrasting pink royal icing on the white cake. The design is also piped on top of the cake. This is a 10-inch (25-cm) petal-shaped cake covered with marzipan and fondant.

How to Make an Eyelet Lace Plaque

1. On a surface lightly dusted with confectioner's sugar, roll out the fondant thinly and place it on a cake board that you've also dusted with confectioner's sugar. Apply the template to the fondant and cut around the scalloped edge, making sure that it is not sticking to the work surface.

2. Use a pin or a scribing tool to carefully prick and mark the design.

3. Remove the paper template and, using a knitting needle or the pointed end of a paintbrush handle, mark the round holes of the design by pressing straight through the fondant. Hold the knitting needle or paintbrush at a 45-degree angle to mark the oval holes.

4. Use a parchment-paper piping bag fitted with a #0 piping tube and filled halfway with royal icing, and pipe around the round and oval holes with fine threads of icing.

5. Pipe the edge of the plaque with a zigzag stitch, buttonhole edging, or petit point.

6. Fill in the remaining design with fine lines and dots.

7. Allow the plaque to dry in a warm place.

8. Carefully slide the plaque onto the cake. Finish the design with fine piping around the edge of the plaque.

Modeling

Marzipan and fondant, being pliable, can be molded like modeling clay into many shapes, such as fruit, vegetables, flowers, and animals. Making these types of decorations is a lot of fun, and you can achieve realistic results if you work with a model in front of you so you can re-create the shapes, colors, and details.

Color each piece of marzipan or fondant to the shade you require, and simply mold each piece into the desired shape. As discussed in the following section, there are many ways to add details for a realistic look.

Modeling Fruit

Apples: Color the marzipan or fondant pale green and roll it into round balls. Make an indentation at the top and bottom of each with the end of a paintbrush. Cut some cloves in half and use the tops for the apple stems and the bases as the calyxes on the bottom of the apples. Use red food coloring to paint in red markings.

Apricots: Color the marzipan or fondant an apricot shade and shape it into small balls. Mark the line on each with the back of a knife and make a slight indentation on the top of each. Using a dusting brush, dust a little pink petal dust on the surface.

Bananas: Color the marzipan or fondant yellow with a touch of brown and make a sausage shape with slightly tapered ends. Bend slightly to curve it along the length and then shape the ridges of the banana with a knife. Paint on the details using a fine paintbrush and brown food coloring.

Grapes: Color the marzipan or fondant a pale green or burgundy and mold it into tiny beads. Assemble these beads into a triangular shape and then build up the layers so that it looks like a bunch of grapes.

Lemons: Mold yellow marzipan or yellow-colored fondant into round balls and then form them into oval shapes with pointed ends. Mark the lemons' skin by rolling the shapes on a fine grater. Press the end of a clove into each for the calyx.

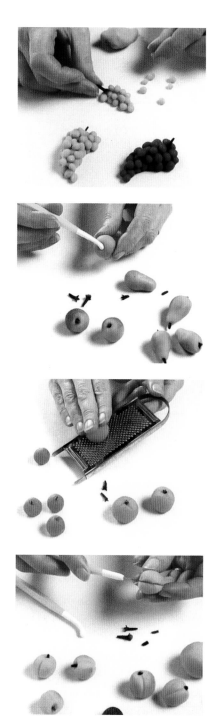

Mandarin oranges: Color the marzipan or fondant a deeper orange than what you would use for the regular orange. Follow the same steps for making oranges, but make the shapes smaller.

Oranges: Color the marzipan or fondant orange and shape it into balls. Mark the oranges' skin by rolling the shapes on a fine grater. Mark a star shape on top of each with the back of a knife and insert the end of a clove into each star for the calyx.

Peaches: Color the marzipan or fondant a pale peach and shape it into small balls with indentations at the tops. Mark the line around each with the back of a knife. Using pink petal dust and a dusting brush, apply the color for the peach bloom.

Pears: Color the marzipan or fondant yellowy green and shape it into balls. Gently shape each ball into a pear shape with your fingers. Make an indentation in the top and bottom of each pear with the end of a paintbrush. Cut some cloves in half and use the tops for the stems and the bases as the calyxes on the bottom of the pears. Paint on markings with brown or red food coloring.

Plums: Color the marzipan or fondant a burgundy color and shape as you did for the apricot but make the shape slightly oval. Mark the line with a knife and press a clove in the top of each for the stem.

Did You Know?
If you are coloring marzipan to mold into decorations, always start with white marzipan.

How to Hand-Model Animals and Figures

Hand-modeling is fun, and using marzipan and fondant enables you to create individual characters with a variety of expressions and characteristics. You can find inspiration almost anywhere, or you can simply use your imagination to create your own characters. Before beginning your adventure with hand-modeling, read the following tips.

- If using marzipan for modeling, use the white variety.
- Always use fresh, pliable marzipan or fondant.
- Do not knead any crusted bits into your marzipan or fondant because this will cause the rest of it to become lumpy and difficult to mold.
- Separate the marzipan or fondant into the number of pieces you require and color them accordingly, kneading them well until evenly colored and smooth. Note that dust or paste colors will give you bright, vibrant colors without affecting the consistency of the marzipan.
- Always work with clean utensils, hands, and work surfaces. Wash your hands frequently throughout the process because they will become sticky. Dry your hands well after washing them; otherwise, the marzipan or fondant will become tacky.
- Dust the work surface and your hands well with confectioner's sugar, but don't use cornstarch when modeling figures because it can encourage mold growth, cracking, and patches in the colored medium.
- Shape the figures or animals piece by piece, assemble them, and mark any details using tools or food-coloring pens.
- Dry the figures in a cardboard cake box in a warm, dry place away from direct sunlight to prevent the colors from fading. Store them this way until you are ready to use them.

How to Model Christmas Pieces

Christmas trees: Mold pieces of green marzipan into cone shapes and, using a pair of scissors, snip marzipan from the cone to make "branches," working around the cone from top to bottom.

Reindeer: Color some marzipan brown and use it to shape an oblong body piece. Make a cut at each end of the body to within half an inch (1 cm) of the center; these will be the front and back legs. Shape the hooves and bend the cut pieces to form front and back legs. Mold a heart-shaped piece for the head and press the top curves of the head into antlers, snipping with scissors to shape. Place the head in position on the body and attach brown ears and a red nose. Use a brown food-coloring pen for the markings.

Sack of presents: Shape a piece of brown marzipan into a ball. Use a modeling tool to hollow out the ball, making the top edge thinner. Shape presents from red and green fondant or marzipan.

Santa Claus: Use red marzipan to cut out and shape a body, a hat, two sleeves, and a red nose. Use white fondant to shape the edging that goes around the base of the body, hat, and sleeves. Press white fondant through a sifter and use it for the beard and hair. Color some fondant to a flesh tone and shape the head and hands. Assemble the parts and secure them using a little egg white or apricot glaze (see page 205). Mark the eyes with a food-coloring pen.

Christmas Cake

The hand-modeled Santa Claus, sack, presents, trees, and reindeer on this Christmas cake were made from marzipan. The 8-inch (20-cm) square cake is covered in marzipan and has a flat top and peaked royal-icing sides. The cake board is trimmed with ribbon.

How to Model Circus Figures

Bucket of foam: Sandwich a round of black fondant between two rounds of green fondant to make the bucket; hollow out the center with a modeling tool. Press some cream-colored fondant through a sifter and fill up the bucket with "foam." Shape the handle from a remnant of the black and green fondant and press in position.

Clown: Place strips of red and black fondant on a rolled-out piece of white fondant. Roll lightly to give a striped effect. Shape an oblong piece of white fondant and then cover it with a strip of striped fondant. Make a cut halfway through to form the body and legs of the clown. Line the inside of the legs with more striped fondant. Shape the arms and ball in the same way: start with white fondant and cover it with striped fondant. Mold and cut out the remaining pieces—red and black frills for the hat and ruffs for the neck, sleeves, and legs. Shape a red mouth, nose, and cone-shaped hat, two black shoes, a flesh-colored head and hands, and a white mask. Use brown fondant pressed through a sifter for the hair. Assemble all the pieces and secure with egg white or apricot glaze.

Elephant: Use dark-gray fondant to shape an oblong body. Make a cut at the front and back of the body to shape into the front and back legs. Shape a cone for the head and elongate the pointed end into a trunk. Shape two gray ears. Roll out small beads of white fondant to make two eyes, two thin tusks, and the detail for the feet. Shape the pink hat and red ribbon from fondant. Fit all of the pieces together and secure them with egg white or apricot glaze.

Seal: Mold black fondant into a cone shape. Shape the pointed end into a head and the rest of the cone into the body and tail. Mold the balls from fondant of different colors.

Circus Cake

A fun cake for any age, this 8-inch (20-cm) round cake is covered with marzipan and white fondant and features hand-modeled decorations. Strips of red and black fondant are positioned diagonally on the white fondant around the side of the cake. Because the fondant was rolled thinly before being placed on the cake, the red and black fondant blended into the white for a striped effect. The thin roll around the perimeter of the top of the cake was made by kneading red, black, and white fondant trimmings together and crimping it into position.

Piping
Techniques

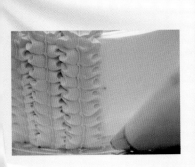

*T*he art of piping is often regarded as difficult to master, but this does not always have to be the case; piping is a valuable cake-decorating skill to have. The keys to success are to practice and have infinite patience. All you need is a good-quality piping bag or parchment-paper piping bag fitted with a straight-sided metal tube. With this simple equipment, you can transform all kinds of icing into stars, shells, flowers, scrolls, lines, and more to create beautiful, professional-looking decorations for all types of cakes.

Piping Equipment

If you practice and adhere to the few guidelines that follow, you'll be amazed at how quickly you will become confident in using a piping bag and tube. Try out simple designs at first to get the feel of using and controlling the piping bag. When you feel ready, try more advanced designs with a few differently shaped tubes. As your skill level increases, you'll be able to work with different types of icing and expand the range of tubes you use.

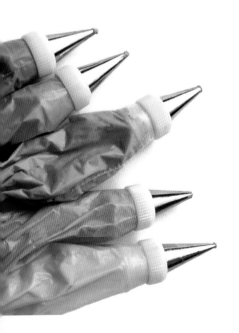

Commercially made piping bags: You can buy piping bags in plastic, vinyl, or washable canvas from cake-decorating retailers, craft stores, or kitchen stores. They are easy to handle and thus good for beginners. They come in a range of sizes and work with all types of icing.

Parchment-paper piping bags: One of the advantages of parchment-paper piping bags is that they can be used with or without icing tubes. To use without a tube, simply fill the bag with icing, fold down the top, and snip off the end of the bag.

If you want to pipe leaves instead of lines, cut a V shape into the end of the bag instead of snipping straight across. You simply throw the bags away after use. Choose good-quality parchment paper for making the bags, and follow the instructions provided later in this chapter.

Icing tubes: Icing tubes come in a seemingly endless array of shapes and sizes. Beginners should start with a small selection of straight-sided metal tubes because they give clean, sharp results. Choose two writing tubes and small, medium, and large star tubes to start. After mastering the use of these tubes, build up your collection as you try new piping designs. Keep them clean and store them carefully in a box or rigid container so they do not get damaged. Always clean icing tubes with a special cleaning brush so that the ends do not become bent or damaged.

How to Make a Parchment-Paper Piping Bag

1. Cut out a 15 × 10-inch (38 × 25-cm) rectangle of parchment paper. Fold it in half diagonally and cut along the fold line to form two triangular shapes, each with a blunt end. Fold the blunt end of the triangle over into the center to make a sharp cone; hold it in position.
2. Fold the sharp end of the triangle over the cone shape. Hold all points together at the back of the cone, making sure that the point of the cone is sharp.
3. Turn the points inside the top edge of the cone and crease firmly. Optional: Secure with tape or staple together.

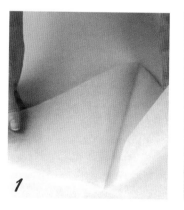

1

2

3

Icing Consistency

Before using any piping equipment, you must make sure that your icing is the correct consistency. If you are using buttercream frosting, it should form a fine, sharp point when you draw a wooden spoon out of the frosting. If the frosting is too stiff, it will be difficult to squeeze out of the bag; if it is too soft, the frosting will be difficult to control, and the piped shapes will rapidly lose their definition.

When piping whipped cream, you need a much softer consistency. Whip the cream until it peaks softly (overwhipping causes curdling and unsightly piping). Once the whipped cream is in the piping bag, it may feel too soft, but the warmth of your hands will cause the cream to thicken and sometimes even to curdle. This is one reason you should fill the piping bag only halfway with whipped cream—so you don't waste too much if this happens.

Piping consistency for buttercream frosting.

Piping consistency for royal icing.

Piping consistency for whipped cream.

Basic Piping Techniques

When piping with any type of icing, it is best to practice piping on a board or work surface before starting on the cake. This also allows you to ensure that the icing is the correct color and consistency.

Start with a parchment-paper, vinyl, or canvas piping bag fitted with a straight-sided metal tube to give a clean, sharp, defined pattern. Fill the bag halfway with icing; do not be tempted to fill it to the top because the fuller an icing bag is, the harder it is to squeeze the icing out of the tube, resulting in aching wrists and hands and poor piping. A good rule of thumb to remember is the smaller the icing tube, the less icing you need.

To pipe royal icing or buttercream frosting, hold the piping bag comfortably with the tube through your first two fingers and thumb, as if you were holding a pencil. Apply pressure at the top of the bag with your other hand. Your wrists and arms should be relaxed, ready to guide the tube.

To pipe whipped cream, it is better to use a nylon piping bag fitted with a larger tube to pipe whipped cream into swirls, shells, or stars. Fill the bag halfway with whipped cream and twist the top of the bag so the cream comes to the end of the tube. Holding the top of the bag with one hand and the tube with the other, gently press out the whipped cream into the desired shape, twisting the bag as it empties.

Simple Piped Shapes

Piping is the obvious choice when decorating a cake, but beginners can be discouraged by complicated piping designs. Choose a simple star icing tube and fit it into a parchment-paper piping bag to pipe stars, swirls, scrolls, and shells. You can make many other types of designs with a plain writing tube.

Star: To pipe a star shape, hold the bag straight above the surface of the cake. Press out the icing, forming a star on the edge of the cake, then pull off to break the icing. Repeat all around the cake to make a neat border.

Swirl: To pipe a swirl, fill the piping bag halfway, fold down the top of the bag, and squeeze the icing until it reaches the end of the tube. Place the icing tube on the surface of the cake, press out the icing, and pipe a swirl of icing in a circular movement. Stop pressing on the bag and pull it up sharply to break the icing. Repeat to pipe swirls around the top edge and base of the cake.

Scroll: To pipe scrolls, hold the piping bag at an angle so the icing tube is almost on its side in front of you. Press out the icing onto the top edge of the cake to secure the scroll. Pipe outward in a circular movement and return the icing tube to the edge of the cake. Stop pressing the bag and break off the icing. Repeat, but this time pipe the icing away from the edge of the cake in the opposite direction in a circular movement and then return the icing tube just to the edge. This is called a reverse scroll, when you pipe one scroll inward and then one outward. For a straight scroll design, pipe the scrolls in one direction only.

Shell: To pipe shells, hold the piping bag at an angle to the cake so the icing tube is almost on its side in front of you. Press out some icing gently and secure it to the surface of the cake. Move the icing tube forward and then move it slowly up, over, and down in what is almost a rocking movement. Stop pressing and break off the icing by pulling the tube toward you. Repeat this process, starting at the end of the first shell to give a shell edging.

Lines: To pipe lines, fit the piping bag with a plain writing tube (the smaller the hole, the finer the lines) and fill it halfway with icing. Pipe a thread of icing, securing the end to the surface of the cake. Continue to pipe the icing just above the surface of the cake, allowing the thread to fall in a straight or curved line. When you've finished the line, stop pressing on the bag and break off the icing.

Trellis: To make a trellis design, pipe parallel lines of icing in one direction and then overpipe them with perpendicular lines. You can pipe the lines straight across or diagonally, depending on the desired end result. Adding a third line across the latticework will result in a more intricate finish.

Dropped-loop threadwork: To create dropped-loop threadwork, use a plain writing tube to pipe a thread of icing, securing the end to the side of the cake. Continue to pipe the icing just away from the side of the cake so the thread forms a loop. Stop pressing when the loop is long enough, join the icing loop to the side of the cake, and break off the icing. Repeat the process, piping more loops. Once you've finished piping loops all around the cake, you might want to overpipe each loop to make them double width or make a slightly longer loop under each existing loop. There are endless possibilities with dropped-loop threadwork.

Leaves: To pipe leaves, fill an uncut parchment-paper piping bag with icing and press the icing to the end of the bag. Cut the end of the piping bag into an inverted V shape. Place the tip of the bag on the surface of the cake, press out the icing to form a leaf shape, and then sharply break off the icing. Repeat to make a pretty border, to make a design, or to decorate flowers.

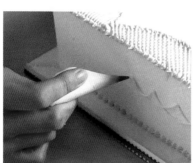

Filigree and cornelli work: For filigree or cornelli work, fit a parchment-paper piping bag with a plain writing tube and fill it halfway with icing. Holding the piping bag like a pencil, pipe threads of icing into W and M shapes, keeping the flow of the icing constant. Remember to work in all directions, not in lines.

Beads and dots: Piping beads or dots of icing is quite simple, but the icing has to be of a softer consistency so the beads don't have sharp points. Trial and error will help you produce icing of the correct consistency. To make beads and dots, fit a parchment-paper piping bag with a #3 plain tube, fill the bag halfway with icing, and fold down the top of the bag. Press the icing out just above the surface of the cake to form a rounded bulb of icing and then pull upward sharply to break off the icing. Repeat to make a border of nicely rounded beads.

Design extension work carefully to complement the shape of the cake and any other decorations included in the design. Other decorations that complement this beautiful technique are lace pieces, tube embroidery, flowers, and ribbon insertion. You also must start with a level cake with straight sides and a coating of smooth fondant or icing free from any blemishes; extension work will not hide flaws in the icing.

The icing that you're using to pipe the extension work must be soft, smooth, and of a light texture that will flow easily through the piping tube; it should be of medium-peak consistency and beaten well. It must also be free of any lumps that could block the piping tube. Adding liquid glucose, or glucose syrup, will give the icing a greater elasticity, which is a great advantage when piping vertical lines. Add ¼ teaspoon (1 ml) of liquid glucose to each egg white and allow the egg whites to sit for twenty-four hours at room temperature before using them to make the icing. Also be sure to sift the confectioners' sugar with a very fine sifter to eliminate any lumps that could block the tube or cause the threads of icing to break.

To make a template for extension work, cut a strip of parchment paper to the perimeter and height of the side of the cake. Fold the strip in half as many times as required to make the paper template the width of the scallop required (usually about 1 inch [2½ cm]). Draw a semicircle at the base of the template and cut it out. Next, cut the top edge of the template to the shape and depth required for the vertical lines.

Hexagonal Wedding Cake

A beautiful centerpiece for any wedding, this 12-inch (30-cm) cake is covered with marzipan and soft-pink fondant and decorated with scalloped extension work and piped embroidery. The arrangement of white freesia with pink ribbons is just enough to enhance this cake.

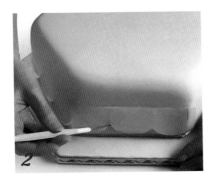

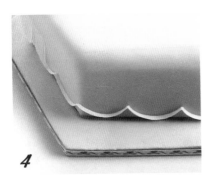

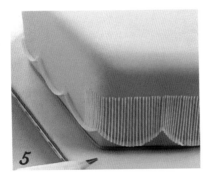

How to Do Extension Work

1. Secure the template around the side of the cake with tape and, using a pin, mark the top edge of the design and the scalloped shape at the base.

2. Place the cake on a turntable so that it is at eye level and tilt it away from you. Using a pin, mark the high points of the scallop design again so that you are sure where the loops start and finish.

3. To work the bridge, touch the cake with the tube at the highest point of the scallop and press out a little icing to attach the thread. Pull the tube just away from the cake and maintain even pressure to pipe the thread, allowing it to follow the scallop line. Touch the scallop at the next highest point on the design. Continue piping and work around the cake, making sure that the first row of bridge work is dry before starting on the second. There should be no gaps between the cake and scallops because this can cause a weak bridge.

4. Pipe each loop exactly over the preceding loop, finishing the thread just slightly shorter on each. Pipe about six loops to build up the bridge and then allow the piping to dry before starting the extension work.

5. To pipe the extension work, tilt the cake toward you so that the lines fall straight. Touch the cake with the tube at the top of the design to attach the thread of icing and pull away immediately, taking care not to form a bulb of icing at the top. Pipe vertical lines just beyond the bridge and then remove the ends with a fine, damp paintbrush. The lines should be parallel and so close together that you cannot pipe another line in between them.

If you are unsure of your writing skills, start with names and greetings formed with carefully spaced capital letters. Pipe the letters in white royal icing first and then overpipe with colored icing.

With practice, you will develop an attractive freehand writing style.

Letters and numbers in the form of run-outs are an alternative decoration to freehand writing.

Writing on a Cake

Writing, or lettering, on a cake can be daunting because you may be worried about making a mistake on a finished cake or because you have not yet developed a distinctive style of writing. With some practice, you will develop a style that is suited to your own hand.

Start by looking at letter samples in cake decorating books or online, and copy a style you like. Write some words on a piece of paper and cover it with a piece of Plexiglas. Using a #1 plain writing tube and royal icing, pipe the letters over and over again in the chosen style and then wipe the Plexiglas clean and start over.

Before writing on a cake, figure out the number of letters in each word and how much space the letters take up so that you can space them evenly on the surface of the cake. If you still feel unsure about the spacing of the letters, trace them on a piece of parchment paper and mark the letters on the cake with a pin. Pipe the letters in white royal icing first and then pipe over them with colored icing to finish the shapes.

You may also make letters in the form of run-outs. There are many styles to choose from, from basic printed letters to fancy Gothic script. Run-out letters may be colored, left plain, or decorated with additional piping when they are completely dry. Additional techniques include floral lettering, with piped flowers on each letter; dotted lettering; and monograms.

Icing Run-Outs

Icing run-outs are one of the most exacting forms of cake decoration. They can be made in any shape or form by simply tracing over a chosen design or pattern. Once made, small run-outs keep well if placed between layers of waxed paper in a box stored in a dry place. So, if you need a quantity of run-outs to decorate a cake, you can make them in advance. Larger run-outs and collars are more difficult to keep because they may warp during storage. Once you make them, allow them to dry completely and then apply them to your cake.

Run-outs are made from royal icing and are very fragile, so it is wise to start with small, solid shapes and make more than you need to allow for breakage. When you are confident at making the simple, solid shapes, practice making finer pieces, figures, and scenes. Accuracy, not speed, is important when making run-outs, so always allow plenty of time.

Royal Icing Consistency

The consistency and texture of the icing must be correct or the run-outs will be difficult to make and handle. Use egg whites or reconstituted egg-white powder with no additives, such as glycerin or lemon juice. The icing should be light and glossy, not heavy and dull. When you lift a spoon from the icing, the icing should form a soft peak that bends over at the tip. This is the proper consistency for piping the outline of the run-outs.

Icing to fill in the run-outs must be soft enough to flow with the help of a paintbrush but able to just hold its shape until tapped, then becoming smooth. Dilute the royal icing with reconstituted egg-white powder, and test a little bit on a flat surface to assess the consistency. If possible, leave the icing to stand overnight, covered with damp cheesecloth, to allow any air bubbles to come to the surface, and then stir the icing until it is completely smooth.

How to Make an Icing Run-Out

Draw or trace the chosen design several times, well spaced apart, on a piece of paper. Place the paper on a flat surface and cover it with a piece of Plexiglas. Cover the design with a piece of waxed paper and secure it to the Plexiglas with tape or icing.

Fit a parchment-paper piping bag with a #0 or #1 writing tube, and fill the bag halfway with soft-peak icing to pipe the outline. Fill several other parchment-paper piping bags halfway with the softer icing, fold down the tops, and leave them for later.

Pipe carefully around the outline of the design with a continuous thread of icing or with as few breaks as possible. To do this, squeeze out a little icing at the least obvious point of the run-out and secure the icing thread to the film or paper. Lift the thread of icing just above the surface and squeeze the bag gently, allowing the thread to fall on the line marking the run-out shape. Join the icing where it started.

Snip the pointed end off one soft-icing bag and fill in the run-out. Start by piping around the inside edge to keep the outline soft; otherwise, it may break. Then work toward the center, filling the shape so the icing looks rounded and overfilled—the icing will shrink as it sets.

Use a fine paintbrush or toothpick to ensure that the area is completely filled in and that the icing is smooth and rounded. Gently tap the board so that any bubbles rise to the surface. If they do, pop them with a pin. For a large run-out, leave it in position on the Plexiglas and allow it to dry. For small run-outs, carefully release the waxed paper or plastic wrap and transfer the run-out to a flat board to dry. Replace the Plexiglas, cover the design with more waxed paper or plastic wrap, and repeat to make as many run-outs as you need. If possible, leave the run-outs under a spotlight to dry their surfaces quickly, because the faster they

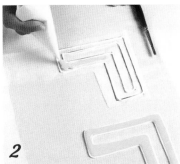

dry, the glossier they will be. Otherwise, leave them in a warm, dry place overnight.

Carefully peel off the paper or plastic from the run-outs and place them on the cake. Secure them in place with small beads or a line of royal icing. If you don't need to use small run-outs right away, you can leave them on the paper or plastic and store them in a cardboard box between layers of waxed paper.

Run-Out Corner Pieces

1. Place the waxed paper or plastic wrap over the sketched design. Pipe the outline of the corner pieces using a #0 plain writing tube and white royal icing.
2. Fill several parchment-paper piping bags halfway with yellow royal icing, snip off the points of the bags, and fill in the corner pieces as quickly and as evenly as possible.
3. When the run-out pieces are completely dry, loosen them very carefully using a thin angled icing spatula.
4. Turn the run-out corner pieces over and pipe fine lines of royal icing from a #0 plain writing tube, working diagonally from edge to edge. Complete the lines in one direction and then pipe in the opposite direction to form a trellis pattern.
5. When the trelliswork is dry, attach the corner pieces to the cake with royal icing.

How to Make a Run-Out Collar

1. Secure the waxed paper or plastic wrap firmly over the collar design with a few beads of royal icing. Pipe the outline of the collar using a #1 plain writing tube and white royal icing.

2. Have several parchment-paper piping bags filled halfway with yellow royal icing. Snip off the point of one bag and begin to fill in the collar, working as quickly and neatly as possible.

3. Use a fine paintbrush to coax the yellow icing to the white icing outline, taking care not to touch the outline with the brush, or the outline may break.

4. Continue to fill in the collar, working from both sides until the collar is completely filled in with yellow icing.

5. When the collar has dried completely, pipe the bead edging and embroidery design on the collar.

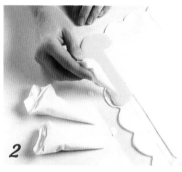

Run-Out Motifs

Run-out piped figures are fun to make. You can make them on waxed paper and then apply them directly to the cake, or you can make them on a sugar plaque and then place the plaque on the cake. These figures look very different from normal run-outs because they take on a three-dimensional appearance with individual sections filled in with different colored icings. When the run-out is dry, you can paint in the details using food-coloring pens or a paintbrush and paste colors; you can also make small additions, such as fondant flowers or piped details.

To get ideas for a figure or a motif, take a look at greeting cards, children's books, wrapping paper, fabrics, and wallpaper patterns. Choose a figure that is simple in shape and not too intricate in detail because you need to complete each section separately by outlining the various sections and filling them in with different colored icings. Alternatively, you can fill in all of the sections with white icing and paint the colors and details by hand when the motif is completely dry.

Once you have drawn your figure, ensure that it's the right size to fit your cake. You may need to enlarge or reduce the picture, which is easy to do with a copier; this also allows you to experiment with various sizes.

1

2

3

How to Make a Run-Out Motif

1. Trace the design, place it on a flat surface, and cover it with a piece of Plexiglas. Cover the Plexiglas with waxed paper or plastic wrap, securing the edges with tape. Alternatively, you could transfer the design onto a sugar plaque, using a pin to mark the design.

2. Make the run-out icing to a slightly thicker consistency, and tint to the colors required for your design. Outlines are not used in this design, so fill in the sections in stages, allowing the surface of each to skin over before filling in adjacent sections; otherwise, the icings will merge and you will lose definition.

3. Pipe the details with a plain writing tube.

4. Use a fine paintbrush to guide the soft icing to fill the shape required.

5. To obtain the different levels of icing in the various sections, you will have to fill in some sections with level icing and fill in other sections full and rounded to obtain the contrast.

6. When the motif is completely filled in, let it dry under a spotlight or in a warm, dry place.

7. Finish the motif by adding the details in the form of piping, painting, or appliqué sugar pieces. The motif should look bright and glossy and include varying textures and levels of icing.

4

5

Motif Cake

Choose a design and transfer it onto a sugar plaque
made from gum paste (see Chapter 9). This 8-inch
(20-cm) cake is covered with marzipan and royal
icing and decorated with ribbons and simple piping in
colors that match the plaque. The recipient can keep
the plaque as a memento of the occasion.

Working with
Gum Paste

um paste is a remarkable medium used mainly for modeling very fine sugar flowers, sugar plaques, and other intricate items. It is exceptionally easy to work with, particularly when rolled out very thinly. You can mold or cut it into flower shapes, and it dries so quickly that the flowers set in such a way that they look almost real. When items made from gum paste dry, they are exceptionally hard, almost like ceramics.

Gum Paste Flowers

Flowers made from gum paste may be wired onto stems and shaped into sprays and bouquets. Gum paste is also wonderful for making plaques of any shape or size, and you can frill or crimp the edges. The finished plaque will be as hard as a ceramic tile, which makes working on it exceptionally easy. You may apply flowers to it, decorate it with piping or food-coloring pens, or paint it with a fine paintbrush.

To make the paste, simply buy the mix and add water. It is, however, expensive in large quantities and therefore should be used with care. There is also a reliable recipe for gum paste later in this book, which is a much more economical way to make a large quantity if you need it.

Once you make gum paste, you must seal it in a plastic bag and use it within a month, or it will become hard and unusable. It is best to make the gum paste a few days before you need it so it is fresh and pliable to work with. You can color or tint gum paste in the usual way with food coloring, or you can dust it with petal dust once it is dry.

Flowers made with plunger cutters are very versatile (you can also use gum-paste cutters or simple cookie

Did You Know?

Working with gum paste requires specialized equipment, including modeling tools (usually sold in sets), calyx cutters, and plunger cutters.

cutters). You can add the flowers, wired or unwired, to frilled edgings, extension work, and border work, or incorporate them into floral sprays.

While you can use fondant with plunger cutters, gum paste is much stronger and holds its shape better, and it is easier to wire gum-paste flowers onto stems to make sprays. If you wish to wire sprays together, you need flowers that have set extra hard so they do not shatter and break while being wired.

Tint or color the gum paste to the shade you require. On a clean, lightly cornstarched surface, roll out the gum paste until it is thin enough that you can see through it. Cut out the flower shape using a large, medium, or small cutter and place it on a piece of dry sponge. Eject the flower by pressing the plunger into the sponge to bend the paste into the shape of the flower. Repeat this process to make a variety of small, medium, and large blossoms.

If the flowers are to have stamens in the center, make a pinhole in each blossom as you make it. When the blossoms are dry, pipe a bead of royal icing on the back of each stamen and thread it through the sugar blossom to secure. Turn the blossoms upside down to dry. When the blossoms are completely dry, store them in a box between sheets of tissue paper or wire them together using fine floral wire to make sprays.

To make blossom plunger flowers into sprays, you will need a length of about 4 inches (10 cm) of 28–30-gauge floral wire and tape for each flower. A good mix for a balanced spray is three large blossoms, four medium blossoms, and five small blossoms; wire the small blossoms at the end of the spray with the medium and large blossoms mixed in.

Make a hook at the end of the wire, place the stamen through the hook, and squeeze it together to secure. Next, attach the floral tape to the back of the blossom and twist it between your fingers to cover about ½ inch (1 cm) of the wire and the stamen. Attach another blossom and continue to wrap the tape around the stems to join the blossoms securely together. When you have added all of the blossoms, continue to wrap the tape around the remaining stems for a neat finish. Store the sprays in a warm, dry place in a box between layers of tissue paper until you need to use them.

Did You Know?

Items made with gum paste are not edible because of the hardness of the paste, so it is better to remove these decorations as keepsakes before cutting the cake.

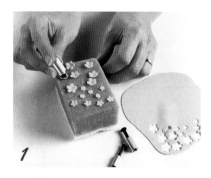

1

2

3

How to Make a Gum Paste Flower Spray

1. Using large, medium, and small blossom plunger cutters, cut out several flower shapes in each size and press them onto a piece of sponge. Make a pinhole in the center of each blossom for the stamen and allow the blossoms to dry.

2. Pipe a bead of royal icing on the back of a stamen and thread it through the hole in the blossom to secure. Repeat with the remaining blossoms and then let them dry upside down.

3. Take a 4-inch (10-cm) length of floral wire and make a hook at one end. Place the hook around the stamen at the back of the blossom and squeeze together to secure. Repeat for the remaining blossoms. Take one wired blossom and bind with floral tape from the back of the blossom and down to cover about ½ inch (1 cm) of the wire and stamen.

4. Add another blossom and continue to wrap the stems with the tape. Continue in this way, adding as many blossoms as you need, and finish by binding the exposed wires with tape.

Blossom Spray Cake

The run-out corner pieces with trelliswork give this royal-iced cake its regal appearance. The center arrangement is made of plunger cutter sprays and ribbon loops along with a few primroses to give the arrangement some height. These were all secured in a ball of fondant and allowed to set; they would make a beautiful keepsake.

Cut-Out Sugar Flowers

Cut-out flowers are simple to make using cutters available in different floral designs, including daisy, rose, sweet pea, lily of the valley, carnation, daffodil, fuchsia, and many more. Leaf cutters and calyx cutters to match specific flowers are also available.

Gum paste, food coloring, 26–28-gauge floral wire, and floral tape are all you need to make cut-out flowers; alternatively, you can apply them directly to the cake without wire. When made with gum paste, the paper-thin petals will look very delicate and realistic.

How to Make a Flower Calyx

1. Select a calyx cutter in a suitable size for the flower you are making.
2. Roll out green gum paste until thin and cut out the calyx shape.
3. Place the calyx on a silicone mat and soften the edges with a bone modeling tool.
4. Thread the calyx onto the back of the flower and secure with a little gum arabic glaze or royal icing.
5. Alternatively, make the calyx using the Mexican-hat method presented later in this chapter.

How to Make a Daisy

1. Roll out some white gum paste thinly on a board lightly sprinkled with cornstarch. Cut out the flower shape using a daisy cutter and make sure the daisy does not stick to the work surface.

2. Frill the petals with a toothpick and place the daisy on a piece of sponge. Press the center to cup the daisy.

3. Take a pea-size piece of dark-green gum paste, make it into a cone shape, and roll out the edges thinly. Use a calyx cutter to cut out the shape.

4. Make a hook at the end of a 3-inch (7½-cm) piece of 26-gauge wire. Dip the wire into gum arabic glaze (see page 200) or apply a bead of royal icing and pull it down through the center of the calyx. Place a small piece of green gum paste over the hook. Place the daisy on the prepared calyx, sticking it in place with glaze or royal icing. Press the center lightly with a bone modeling tool to secure.

5. To make the flower center, take a pea-size piece of dark-yellow gum paste and press it onto a sifter to pattern the surface. Attach the flower center to the daisy with gum arabic glaze and dust lightly around the base of the petals with moss-green petal dust.

Good Luck Cake

This horseshoe-shaped cake is covered with marzipan and a warm-yellow fondant finish. The edges are neatly crimped, and the top is decorated with a variety of cut-out sugar flowers, including roses and primroses.

How to Make a Rose

1. Make a hook at the end of a piece of 26-gauge floral wire and dip it in gum arabic glaze. Mold a cone of gum paste around the hook and allow it to dry.
2. Roll out some gum paste thinly on a board lightly dusted with cornstarch, and cut out three shapes in three sizes using a rose cutter.
3. Using a modeling tool, roll the petals to soften.
4. Thread one petal onto the wired cone, secure it with glaze, and then secure the second and third petals so that each is around and over the first.
5. Cut out a green calyx using a rose-shaped calyx cutter and brush it with gum arabic glaze. Thread the rose through the calyx and secure in position. Mold a tiny piece of green paste into a cone, thread it onto the wire, and secure it to the calyx.
6. Optional: Dust with petal dust to highlight the rose.

How to Make a Sweet Pea

1. Make a hook at the end of a 26-gauge floral wire, dip it into gum arabic glaze, and cover it with a tiny piece of gum paste.

2. Roll out a piece of gum paste thinly on a board dusted with cornstarch, and cut out a petal using the smallest sweet-pea cutter. Brush it with a little glaze and fold it around the center cone. Press together to form a flat, semicircular petal shape.

3. Cut out a medium petal and a large petal. Soften the edges and cup each side of the petals with a modeling tool. Attach the medium-size petal to the first petal with glaze so that it looks like a butterfly. Attach the largest petal behind the medium-size petal.

4. Cut out a green calyx using a sweet-pea calyx cutter. Thread it through the cone and attach it to the sweet pea with glaze.

5. Hook the end and hang the flower upside down to dry.

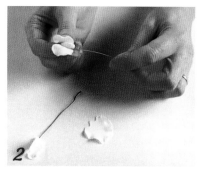

2

3

6

How to Make a Carnation

1. Roll out a piece of colored paste thinly on a board dusted with cornstarch. Cut out several flower shapes using a carnation cutter.

2. Using a modeling knife, make small cuts at intervals around the edges of the petals. Frill the edges using a toothpick, turning the gum paste while working and applying lots of pressure to obtain the very fine edges.

3. Make a hook at the end of a piece of 26-gauge wire. Tape the end of the hook with green floral tape and continue to cover the stem. Carefully place the wire through the center of one petal.

4. Very lightly brush half of the circle with gum arabic glaze and fold to make a semicircle. Brush half the petal again with glaze and fold one-third of it over. Turn the petal over and repeat on the other side.

5. Mold the base of the petal very gently onto the wire, hook the end, and hang it up to dry.

6. Thread two more petals separately onto the wire, brushing each with glaze so they fall into a natural shape. Gently mold the bases and leave them to dry upside down.

Molded or Pulled Flowers

Hand-molded or pulled flowers are basically simple flowers made without cutters, and they are less complicated to make than cutter flowers. You can make small blossoms and use them individually or in sprays to include in a pretty bouquet or arrangement.

The basic equipment required for molded and pulled flowers is a cone-shaped modeling tool, a modeling knife or scissors, some floral wire, and food coloring or petal dust. Most of the flowers are made with four to six petals. To make modeled or pulled flowers, copy real blossoms or pictures; use a cone of gum paste and a flower center modeling tool to make the shape and then press and pull the petals to match the blossom.

To wire these flowers, make a hook at the end of a 28-gauge wire, dip it into gum arabic glaze (see page 200), and pull it through the center of the flower. Mold the paste to the stem and dry upside down. When dry, dust the flowers with petal dust, if desired, and wire them into sprays.

How to Make a Pulled Blossom

1. Take a pea-sized piece of paste and make a cone shape. Dust the modeling tool with cornstarch and insert it into the thick end of the cone shape.
2. Either cut against the cone with a modeling knife or remove it and cut it with scissors to make five evenly sized petals.
3. Open up the flower by gently pressing the petals backward. Shape one petal at a time, pressing it between your thumb and finger to flatten the shape. Pinch the end of the petal to round it slightly and then soften and thin the petal by gently pulling it with your thumb on top and forefinger underneath. Repeat this action with each petal, keeping the petals even in size.

How to Make a Molded Rose

1. Make a cone shape of fondant or gum paste. Press out each petal individually and wrap it around the cone shape, covering it at the top with the first petal. Add a second petal so that the joint of the first petal is in the center of the second petal.
2. Keep adding more petals, gently shaping and curling the edges to give it a realistic shape. Work the rose off the cone shape, using your forefingers to roll the stem thinly enough to separate the rose from the cone.
3. When the rose is dry, gently brush the petals with petal dust to give a hint of color.

 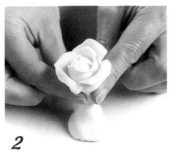 

Mexican-Hat Flowers

This method of making flowers is, in effect, a combination of the pulled blossom and cut-out techniques already described. It can be applied to various types of flower shapes and can be used for making calyxes, too. The results are very effective.

How to Make a Primrose

1. Mold a piece of pale-yellow gum paste into a cone shape and press out the edges thinly, keeping the center cone thin. Place it upside down on an acrylic board. Using a thin modeling tool, lightly roll all the way around the cone to make the circle very thin, with a fine cone shape in the center.
2. Place a primrose cutter over the cone and onto the paste, and cut out the shape.
3. Remove the cutter, hold the cone in one hand, and press a pointed modeling tool with a ridged side into the center of the cone to shape the flowers. Soften the petals with a bone modeling tool on a silicone mat with the cone end in the hole. Leave upside down on a dry sponge to dry.
4. If you are inserting wire or stamens, insert a hooked wire dipped in glaze (see page 200). If the flowers are very delicate, mold a tiny piece of gum paste around the wire before inserting it. Leave the flowers upside down to dry and then color with petal dust.

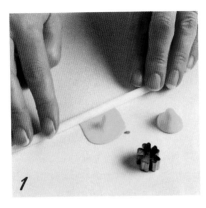

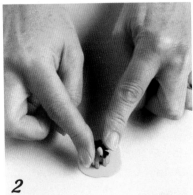

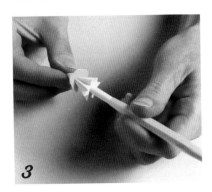

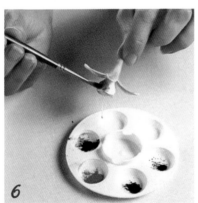

How to Make a Fuchsia

1. Take four pink stamens and fold three in half, keeping one longer. Wrap a fine piece of wire around the stamens and attach them securely to a length of 30-gauge wire with green floral tape.

2. Roll out a piece of gum paste very thinly and cut out five petal shapes with a small, petal-shaped cutter. Brush the edges of each with gum arabic glaze and arrange them in a line, each one overlapping the other slightly.

3. Shape a piece of gum paste into a cone. Press the wide end flat, keeping a thin cone shape in the center. Place the cone on an acrylic board and, using a thin modeling tool, roll out the edges until very thin, keeping the cone in the center thin enough to place the fuchsia cutter over. Cut out the cone shape with the fuchsia cutter, and make a cavity in the center of the cone with the thin modeling tool.

4. Loosely roll up the group of five petals, pressing the pointed ends together to make a petal cone. Thread the stamens through the center and brush the necks of the stamens with glaze. Press to fit around the wire and hang upside down to dry for ten minutes.

5. Place the fuchsia cone into the hole on the silicone mat. Soften and curl the petals with a bone modeling tool. Brush the center with glaze and carefully thread the stamen wire through the center of the petals to fit firmly.

6. Bend each petal slightly backward to give a realistic appearance. Hang the flower upside down to dry and then dust the flower with pink and purple petal dust.

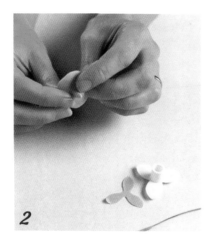

2

3

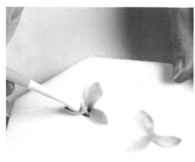

4

How to Make a Freesia Spray

1. Bend two stamens in half and attach them to a piece of 26-gauge floral wire. Secure them with floral tape and cut off the stamen ends.

2. To make the freesia flowers, use a small ball of gum paste shaped into a cone, and press the edges very thinly to look like a hat with a point in the center that is slim enough for the freesia cutter to cover. Place the cutter over the cone and cut out the shape neatly.

3. Press a thin modeling tool into the center of the flower to make a hollow cone shape. Roll out a small piece of gum paste thinly and cut out a flat petal shape with the same cutter.

4. Place the shapes on a silicone mat with the cone shape in the hole so the cone does not get damaged while you are working the petals. Soften the edge and center of each petal with a bone modeling tool, gently curling, enlarging, and cupping the petal shapes.

5. Take the cone-shaped petal and brush the center with a little gum arabic glaze. Place the remaining petal on top so the petals fall in between the cone petals. Thread the stamens carefully through the center, brushing the top stamens with glaze. Pull through so only the

5

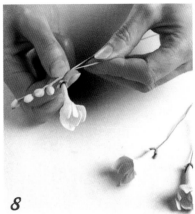

8

stamens and no wire show inside the freesia.

6. Bend the petals carefully and hang the flower upside down to dry. Cut out a tiny star calyx and place it over the end of the flower.

7. Mold a tiny piece of paste into an elongated shape to make the closed buds. Repeat to make three more buds, each larger than the one before. Make a hole in the base of each bud, dip four stamens into the glaze, and insert each into the buds. Let dry.

8. To wire into a spray, use a piece of 30-gauge wire. Start with the tiniest buds and attach them to the end of the wire with tape. Add the remaining buds, positioning them in a line, with a little space between each of them, and securing them with tape. Continue adding the flowers to complete the spray and then bend the wire to its natural shape.

Floral Spray Cake

This simple cake is covered with marzipan and champagne-colored fondant, trimmed with ribbons, and adorned with a spray of handmade sugar flowers.

Leaves

There are two methods of making leaves. The method you use will depend on whether you want flat cut-out leaves or want to wire leaves to add to sprays of flowers.

How to Make Cut-Out and Wired Leaves

1. Color the gum paste the proper shade of green for the type of leaves you are making.
2. For unwired leaves, roll the paste out very thinly. Cut out leaves using leaf cutters or cut around a real leaf. For wired leaves, roll the paste out thinly from each side of the center to form a central ridge. Position the leaf cutter so the ridge runs down the center of the leaf, and cut out the shape.
3. For both types of leaves, make vein impressions by either pressing real leaves onto the paste or using a modeling tool to draw veins on the paste.

4. For unwired leaves, bend the cutouts slightly and dry them over a dowel to impart a curved shape. For wired leaves, dip a 3-inch (7.5-cm) length of 28-gauge floral wire in gum arabic glaze (see page 200) and insert it into the ridge on the back of the leaf. Bend the leaf a little to soften the edges and then allow it to dry.

5. For a more natural effect, brush the leaves with petal dust to variegate the color.

How to Make a Blossom Spray

1. Make a small hook at the end of a length of 28-gauge floral wire and attach a wired leaf. Secure it in position with a piece of floral tape by twisting it with your fingers. Next, add a blossom spray about 1 inch (2.5 cm) down the wire and continue to tape the spray to the wire.

2. Select the wired sugar flowers you want to use and attach these flowers, one at a time, to the wire and secure them with the tape.

3. Gently bend the heads of each flower to create a pleasing arrangement; always use tweezers to bend the wire.

4. Finish the spray of flowers, making sure it lies flat on the surface, and bend the tail into a coil or loop.

Pastillage

Once you've mastered working with gum paste, working with pastillage will be a natural extension of your skills. Pastillage is another type of sugar paste that sets quickly and dries even harder than gum paste. Made of confectioner's sugar, gelatin, cornstarch, and egg white, pastillage is so strong and dries so hard that it can often be mistaken for fine porcelain. Rolling out the paste thinly and cutting very accurately, you can make the paste into delicate plaques, cards, boxes, or molded items.

All of your sugarcraft skills can be combined to make a pastillage plaque. Once you've established and cut out the shape, you may frill or crimp the edges or pipe the plaque with embroidery or eyelet lace edging. The plaque can include molded or cut-out flowers, run-outs, or appliqué work, or you can paint it by hand or write an inscription on it; it may even include modeled figures. Once the plaque is complete, you can place it on a cake as the main decoration or package it in a pretty box and present it as a gift.

To make a pastillage plaque, roll out the paste thinly on a clean surface lightly dusted with cornstarch. Cut out the plaque shape on the surface on which it is to be dried using a sharp knife wielded with a single rocking movement. Do not drag the knife through the paste, or it will stretch the paste. Cut in from the corners—not out, because this may cause them to curl up when dry. For small cuts, use round or oval cutters dipped in cornstarch, pressing down firmly once with the cutter to cut out the shape cleanly. Smooth the edge with your fingers.

Create the desired finish (plain, crimped, eyelet lace, or another design) for the edge of the plaque and then allow it to dry for at least twelve hours. Remember, you must cut out and work on the plaque on the surface on which you will dry it; once you've cut out the shape, you must not move it until it is dry, or it might become distorted.

1

2

Plan the design for the plaque; ideas include run-outs or motifs, handmade sugar flowers, molded items, handwritten or piped inscriptions, and the list goes on. Attach items to the plaque with royal icing and either allow the plaque to dry overnight or place it directly on the iced cake.

How to Make a Pastillage Plaque Decorated with Flowers

1. Make a 6-inch (15-cm) pastillage plaque and crimp the edges.
2. Mold two roses in full bloom and one rosebud and brush them with peach petal dust when dry. Make three daisies, four primroses, two sprays of blossoms, four leaves, and a few ribbon loops.
3. Secure a piece of fondant the size of a walnut in the center of the plaque. Arrange the flowers and ribbons until you are happy with how they look. Press all of the flowers into the fondant, cutting the wires to length, and secure the leaves with a little royal icing.
4. Brush the plaque lightly with peach petal dust.

Floral Plaque Cake

A floral plaque suits almost any special-occasion cake, and, as a bonus, it may be kept afterward as a memento.

Working with Gum Paste *189*

Basic Recipes and Helpful Hints

*N*o amount of icing or decorating skill can disguise a poorly made cake or icing; cakes, after all, are meant to be as delicious as they are attractive. Armed with the tried-and-true recipes presented in this chapter for classic and popular icings and frostings, you should have consistently good results every time. Also included is a wealth of information on storing cakes, planning your time, and more.

Cake-Making Equipment

For successful cake making, you will need a range of items, many of which you may already have in the kitchen. Add to the basics gradually as your skills—and ambitions—progress, and be sure to choose good-quality equipment that will last.

Scale
An accurate scale for weighing ingredients is essential for good results.

Measuring cup (liquids)
Choose an all-purpose cup that measures liquids in ounces, milliliters, and pints.

Measuring cups (dry ingredients)
These cups come in different sizes and give consistently accurate measurements for dry ingredients.

Standard measuring spoons
Measuring spoons can be used for both dry and liquid ingredients.

Wooden spoons
Have a few wooden spoons with handles of varying lengths on hand for mixing.

Whisks
You'll need a small, handheld rotary whisk as well as a wire whisk for whisking cream, egg whites, or light mixtures to increase volume and give smooth consistencies.

Handheld electric mixer
This type of mixer is invaluable when making large quantities of cake batter or icings.

Food processor
A food processor is ideal for chopping ingredients quickly, beating buttercream frosting, and making cake mixtures.

Spatulas
Spatulas with flexible plastic or rubber blades come in many shapes and sizes and are essential for folding ingredients into mixtures and cake batters.

Bowls
Get a selection of small, medium, and large heatproof bowls (glass is a good choice) with smooth, rounded sides to allow thorough, even mixing.

Baking pans and molds
Choose sturdy, good-quality pans for baking. Thicker metal prevents overcooking and ensures that cakes retain their shapes.

Baking sheets
Select heavy-duty baking sheets that will not warp in the oven. Baking sheets without raised edges are preferable for baking, but baking sheets with sides are ideal for standing cake pans on.

Cooling racks
Metal cooling racks come in different sizes and shapes with wide or narrow mesh.

Parchment paper
Parchment paper is good for lining baking pans, making meringues, spreading melted chocolate, and drying molded or cut-out sugar decorations.

Waxed paper
Waxed paper, being thin and flexible, is ideal for icing run-outs and piped decorations.

Glazing brushes
Select small- and medium-size brushes for brushing pans and molds with butter or oil. You'll also need a larger one for brushing cakes with apricot glaze.

Cutters
Plain and fancy cookie cutters are available in many shapes and sizes for cutting shapes out of icing and marzipan. Plain round and fluted pastry cutters are also useful.

Icing spatulas
You'll need both straight and angled icing spatulas with flexible blades for loosening cakes from pans and for spreading and smoothing icing.

Knives
Sharp knives in different sizes come in handy for preparing ingredients and for cutting cakes into layers.

Ruler, scissors, and pencil
These tools are necessary for making accurate measurements.

Cake boards
Cake boards are available in many sizes and shapes, so you can select the right type of board for your cake. Use thick cake boards for large iced cakes and multiple-tiered cakes, and thin cake boards for light cakes with buttercream or whipped cream frosting.

Boxes
Cardboard cake boxes have many uses, including storing and transporting cakes, drying icing and decorations, and storing finished decorations for later use.

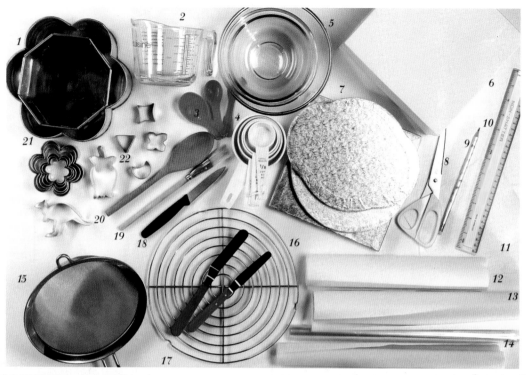

Baking Equipment: 1. Baking pans, **2.** Measuring cup (liquids), **3.** Standard measuring spoons, **4.** Measuring cups (dry ingredients), **5.** Glass heatproof bowls, **6.** Cake box, **7.** Cake boards, **8.** Scissors, **9.** Pencil, **10.** Ruler, **11.** Rice paper, **12.** Waxed paper, **13.** Parchment paper, **14.** Plastic wrap, **15.** Sifter, **16.** Cooling rack, **17.** Icing spatula, **18.** Sharp knife, **19.** Glazing brush, **20.** Wooden spoon, **21.** Pastry cutters, **22.** Fancy cookie cutters.

Frosting and Icing Recipes

Many different types of icing and frosting have been mentioned in the preceding chapters; here are the recipes. These are tried-and-true recipes, so if you follow the instructions and quantities carefully, you will have the perfect medium for practicing your icing and decorating skills.

Chocolate Frosting

This rich, glossy icing sets like chocolate fudge, yet it is versatile enough to coat smoothly, swirl, or pipe, depending on its temperature when used.

To coat and fill an 8-inch (20-cm) cake:

> *4 ounces or 4 squares (125 g) semisweet chocolate*
>
> *2 ounces or ¼ cup (50 g) unsalted butter*
>
> *1 egg, beaten*
>
> *6 ounces or 1½ cups (175 g) confectioners' sugar, sifted*

1. Place the chocolate and butter in a heatproof bowl set over a saucepan of hot water. Stir occasionally with a wooden spoon until melted.
2. Add the egg and beat until smooth. Remove the bowl from the saucepan. Stir in the confectioners' sugar and then beat until smooth and glossy.
3. Pour immediately over the cake for a smooth finish, or allow the icing to cool for a thicker spreading or piping consistency.

Buttercream Frosting

This classic frosting is simple to make and is a fluffy, light addition to any cake. It's easily adaptable to different flavors and colors—the options are endless.

To coat and fill an 8-inch (20-cm) cake:

> 4 ounces or ½ cup (125 g) unsalted
>   butter, softened
> 8 ounces or 2 cups (225 g)
>   confectioners' sugar, sifted
> 2 teaspoons milk
> 1 teaspoon vanilla extract

1. Place the butter in a bowl and beat until light and fluffy using a wooden spoon or electric mixer.
2. Stir in the confectioners' sugar, milk, and vanilla extract until evenly mixed and then beat the icing well until light and smooth.

Variations

Citrus	Replace the milk and vanilla extract with orange, lemon, or lime juice and 2 teaspoons of finely grated orange, lemon, or lime zest (omit the zest if you plan to pipe the icing).
Chocolate	Add 1 tablespoon of cocoa powder blended with 1 tablespoon of boiling water, cooled.
Coffee	Add 2 teaspoons of instant coffee blended with 1 teaspoon of boiling water, cooled.

Flavorings

Coffee	Replace the molasses with 1 tablespoon of instant coffee.
Chocolate	Sift 1 tablespoon of cocoa powder with the confectioners' sugar.
Citrus	Replace the molasses with light corn syrup and add 2 teaspoons of finely grated orange, lemon, or lime zest

Quick Frosting

With brown sugar and molasses, this richly flavored frosting is useful for quickly coating any cake with a smooth or swirled finish.

To coat and fill an 8-inch (20-cm) cake:

3 ounces or ⅓ cup (75 g) unsalted butter

3 tablespoons milk

1 ounce or 2 tablespoons (25 g) light brown sugar

1 tablespoon molasses

12 ounces or 3 cups (350 g) confectioners' sugar, sifted

1. Place the butter, milk, brown sugar, and molasses in a heatproof bowl over a saucepan of simmering water. Using a wooden spoon, stir occasionally until the butter and brown sugar have melted.
2. Remove the bowl from the saucepan. Stir in the confectioners' sugar and then beat until smooth and glossy.
3. Immediately pour the frosting over the cake for a smooth finish, or allow the frosting to cool for a thicker spreading consistency.

Marzipan

Homemade marzipan always has that special flavor and texture that is often missing from packaged marzipan, so it is well worth taking the time to make your own.

To make 1 pound (450 g):

8 ounces or 2¼ cups (225 g) ground almonds
4 ounces or ½ cup (125 g) superfine sugar
4 ounces or 1 cup (125 g) confectioners' sugar, sifted
1 teaspoon lemon juice
1 large egg white
Several drops almond extract

1. Combine the ground almonds and both sugars in a medium-size bowl and stir until evenly mixed.
2. Make a "well" in the center of the mixture and add the lemon juice, almond extract, and enough egg white to mix to a soft but firm dough with a wooden spoon.
3. Lightly dust the work surface with sifted confectioners' sugar and knead the marzipan until smooth and free from cracks.

To store: Wrap the marzipan tightly in plastic wrap and then seal in a resealable plastic bag. Store in the refrigerator for up to one month or in the freezer for up to one year.

Did You Know?

If you're tinting fondant at home, knead food coloring into a small piece of fondant until it is darker than the desired color. Then knead the colored piece into a quantity of white fondant until you've achieved the correct color, the color is even, and the fondant is smooth.

Fondant

Homemade fondant is easy to make and is tastier than the store-bought variety. Fondant is perfect for decorating cakes and can be rolled and shaped, turning small pieces into accents that are limited only by the cake decorator's imagination.

To make about 4 ounces or 1 pound (575 g):

1 egg white
2 tablespoons liquid glucose
2 teaspoons rose water
1 pound or 4 cups (450 g) confectioners' sugar, sifted, plus more to dust

Fondant and Marzipan: How Much Do You Need?

Square Cake	Round Cake	Fondant/Marzipan Quantity
5 inches (13 cm)	6 inches (15 cm)	1 lb (450 g)
6 inches (15 cm)	7 inches (18 cm)	1 lb 8 oz (675 g)
7 inches (18 cm)	8 inches (20 cm)	1 lb 12 oz (800 g)
8 inches (20 cm)	9 inches (23 cm)	1 lb 12 oz (800 g)
9 inches (23 cm)	10 inches (25 cm)	1 lb 12 oz (800 g)
10 inches (25 cm)	11 inches (28 cm)	1 lb 12 oz (800 g)
11 inches (28 cm)	12 inches (30 cm)	3 lb 8 oz (1.6 kg)
12 inches (30 cm)	13 inches (33 cm)	4 lb (1.8 kg)

1. Place the egg white, liquid glucose, and rose water in a clean bowl and mix together to break up the egg white.
2. Add the confectioners' sugar and mix with a wooden spoon until the icing begins to bind together.
3. Knead with your fingers until the mixture forms into a ball and then place it on a surface lightly dusted with confectioners' sugar. Knead until smooth and free from cracks.
4. If the icing is too soft to handle and is sticky, knead in some more sifted confectioners' sugar until firm and pliable. If the fondant dries out and becomes hard, knead in a little boiled and cooled water until the icing is soft and pliable.

To store: Wrap the fondant tightly in plastic wrap or and then place in a resealable plastic bag.

Gum Paste

Gum paste is used only for making cake decorations. It is exceptionally strong and can be molded into very fine flowers or cut into individual sugar pieces that dry very quickly. You can purchase it commercially in a ready-to-mix powdered form or ready-made; the latter is very convenient for small quantities but is rather expensive when needed in large quantities.

To make ½ pound (225 g):

> 8 ounces or 2 cups (225 g) icing confectioners' sugar, sifted
>
> 1 tablespoon gum tragacanth, sifted
>
> 1 rounded teaspoon liquid glucose
>
> 1 tablespoon cold water

1. Sift the confectioners' sugar and gum tragacanth into a bowl.
2. Make a "well" in the center and add the liquid glucose and water.
3. Mix together with your fingers to form a soft paste and then knead on a surface dusted well with confectioners' sugar until smooth, white, and free from cracks.

To store and use: Place the gum paste in a resealable plastic bag and then put the bag in an airtight container. It will keep for up to one month. Allow the gum paste to sit for two hours before using, and then knead it again. Use small pieces at a time, leaving the remaining gum paste well sealed. Use a little vegetable shortening instead of confectioners' sugar when kneading, rolling out, or molding the gum paste to prevent it from becoming dry and to make it more pliable and easier to handle.

Gum Arabic Glaze

This is much better than egg white for sticking flower petals together or securing fondant items. It dries quickly and sets the gum paste.

> 1 tablespoon gum arabic
>
> 3 tablespoons warm water

Blend the gum arabic with the water until smooth and free from lumps. Place in a clean jar and seal with a clean lid. Use as needed.

Royal Icing

Royal Icing Made with Powdered Egg Whites

You may use powdered egg whites in place of fresh egg whites for royal icing. Simply blend the powder with water to reconstitute it as directed, and then add the confectioners' sugar. The powder is easy to use, it doesn't waste fresh egg yolks, and it produces a light, glossy, easy-to-work-with royal icing. This icing is suitable for flat or peaked icing, piping, and run-outs. When used as flat icing for tiered cakes, it sets hard enough to support the weight of the cakes but still cuts easily without being brittle. Do not add the confectioners' sugar too quickly, or you will end up with a dull, heavy icing that will be difficult to handle.

To make 1 pound or 3½ cups (450 g):

1 tablespoon powdered egg whites, sifted

6 tablespoons lukewarm water

1 pound or 4 cups (450 g) confectioners' sugar, sifted

1. Sift the powdered egg whites into a clean bowl. Using a clean wooden spoon, gradually stir in the water and blend together until the liquid is smooth and free from lumps.

2. Mix in enough confectioners' sugar to attain the consistency of unwhipped cream by adding small quantities of confectioners' sugar every few minutes until you've reached the desired consistency, mixing well and gently beating after each addition. The icing should be smooth, glossy, and light—almost like a cold meringue in texture but not aerated.

3. Allow the icing to settle before using it. Cover the surface with a piece of plastic wrap and seal well, expelling all air.

4. Stir the icing thoroughly before use to disperse the air bubbles. Adjust the consistency, if necessary, by adding more sifted confectioners' sugar or powdered egg whites. Alternatively, for large quantities of royal icing, use an electric mixer on the lowest speed.

Royal Icing: How Much Do You Need?

It is always difficult to estimate how much royal icing you will need to ice a cake. The quantity will depend on how you apply the icing, how many layers of icing you're working with, and how thick the layers of icing are. You also have to take the design into consideration whether you are piping a design or creating a number of run-outs and sugar pieces.

The best guide to follow when icing cakes is to make the royal icing in small batches using 2 pounds (900 g) of confectioners' sugar, which is double the quantity of the recipes given here. In this way, you know that each batch of icing is fresh and free from any impurities that may occur when you make a larger quantity of royal icing for one cake. It also helps you assess how much more icing you will need to finish the cake.

The following table is a guide for covering cakes with two or three thin layers of flat royal icing.

Square Cake	Round Cake	Fondant/Marzipan Quantity
5 inches (13 cm)	6 inches (15 cm)	1 lb (450 g)
6 inches (15 cm)	7 inches (18 cm)	1 lb 8 oz (675 g)
7 inches (18 cm)	8 inches (20 cm)	2 lb. (900 g)
8 inches (20 cm)	9 inches (23 cm)	2 lb. 8 oz. (1.1 kg)
9 inches (23 cm)	10 inches (25 cm)	3 lb. (1.4 kg)
10 inches (25 cm)	11 inches (28 cm)	3 lb. 8 oz. (1.6 kg)
11 inches (28 cm)	12 inches (30 cm)	4 lb. (1.8 kg)
12 inches (30 cm)	13 inches (33 cm)	4 lb. 8 oz. (2 kg)

Royal Icing Made with Fresh Egg Whites

This icing is traditionally used to cover cakes and can be used for flat or peaked icing, run-outs, or piped designs. Do not add the confectioners' sugar too quickly, or you will end up with a dull, heavy icing that will be difficult to handle.

Note: When making royal icing for run-outs, omit the glycerin.

To make 1 pound or 3½ cups (450 g):

2 large egg whites

¼ teaspoon lemon juice

1 pound or 4 cups (450 g) confectioners' sugar, sifted

1 tsp glycerin

1. Place the egg whites and lemon juice in a clean bowl. Using a clean wooden spoon, stir thoroughly to break up the egg whites.
2. Mix in enough confectioners' sugar to give the mixture the consistency of unwhipped cream. Continue mixing and add small quantities of confectioners' sugar every few minutes until you've achieved the desired consistency, mixing well and gently beating after each addition. The icing should be smooth, glossy, and light, almost like a cold meringue in texture but not aerated. Stir in the glycerin until the icing is well blended.
3. Allow the icing to settle before using it. Cover the surface with a piece of plastic wrap and seal well, expelling all air.
4. Stir the icing thoroughly before use to disperse the air bubbles. Adjust the consistency, if necessary, by adding more sifted confectioners' sugar. Alternatively, for large quantities of royal icing, use an electric mixer on the lowest speed.

Instant Royal Icing

This is an instant icing used for quickly coating and finishing the tops of cakes. Add an extra flourish by introducing a different color and, using a parchment-paper piping bag and toothpick, create a feathered effect (see page 42).

To coat the top of an 8-inch (20-cm) cake:

> 8 ounces or 2 cups (225 g) confectioners' sugar
> 2–3 tablespoons hot water

1. Sift the confectioners' sugar into a bowl. Using a wooden spoon, gradually stir in enough water to make a mixture similar to the consistency of thick cream.
2. Beat the mixture until the icing is white and smooth and thickly coats the back of a wooden spoon. Color with a few drops of food coloring, if desired.
3. Use immediately to cover the top of the cake.

Variations

To flavor instant royal icing, replace the water with a strong solution of instant coffee for coffee flavor or with freshly squeezed orange, lemon, or lime juice for citrus flavor. For chocolate icing, sift 2 teaspoons of cocoa powder with the confectioners' sugar.

Apricot Glaze

It is always a good idea to make a large quantity of apricot glaze because it keeps in the refrigerator for up to two months and has many uses in cake decorating. Use it for brushing a cake before applying marzipan, glazing fruits for decoration, securing pieces together, and more.

To make 1 pound or 3½ cups (450 g):
> *1 pound or 3½ cups (450 g) apricot jam*
> *3 tablespoons water*

1. Place the jam and water in a saucepan and heat gently, stirring occasionally until melted.
2. Boil rapidly for one minute and then strain through a sieve. Using a wooden spoon, rub through as much of the fruit as possible. Discard the skins left in the sieve.

To store: Pour the glaze into a clean, hot jar. Seal with a clean lid and allow to cool. You can refrigerate the glaze for up to two months.

Caramel

Caramel is the golden brown syrup produced by boiling sugar syrup to an extremely high temperature. It has endless uses for dipping fruit and nuts and for decorating. When it is set and hardened, you can crush it and use it for coating the sides of cakes, or you can break it into pieces and use them as decorations.

To coat the sides of an 8-inch (20-cm) cake:
> *¼ pint or ⅔ cup (150 ml) water*
> *6 ounces or ⅔ cup (175 g) superfine sugar*

1. Place the water in a saucepan and bring to a boil. Remove the saucepan from the heat and stir in the sugar. Heat gently until the sugar has completely dissolved.
2. Bring to a boil again and boil rapidly for several minutes until the bubbles begin to subside and the syrup begins to turn a pale golden brown. Watch carefully at this stage because the syrup will continue to darken when you remove it from the heat.
3. When the caramel is a rich golden brown, it has reached the ideal state for use. Allow the bubbles to subside and then use as needed.

Cutting Cakes

Figuring out the number of servings you'll get from a round or square cake is simple; of course, it depends on whether you intend to serve small slivers or more substantial slices. As a general rule of thumb for round and square cakes, cut from edge to edge into slices, not wedges, about 1 inch (2½ cm) thick. Then cut each slice into 1½-inch (4-cm) pieces. Using these measurements, it is easy to calculate the number of portions you can cut from any given size of cake. On a round cake, the slices become smaller at the curved edges, and the first and last slices of the cake are mainly marzipan and icing, so keep this in mind when calculating servings.

Cake Portion Guide

Cake Size	Round Cake Portions	Square Cake Portions
5 inches (13 cm)	16	20
6 inches (15 cm)	25	30
7 inches (18 cm)	36	42
8 inches (20 cm)	45	56
9 inches (23 cm)	64	72
10 inches (25 cm)	81	90
11 inches (28 cm)	100	120
12 inch (30 cm)	120	140

Schedules for Cake Making

How much time should you allow for making a special-occasion cake? I find the best way is to work backward from the date that you need the finished cake. Here are a few tips.

- Aim to finish the cake a week before it is needed.
- Calculate how long it will take you to make the decorations and apply them to the cake. For example, add an extra week for intricate run-out collars to allow for drying time or if you are making hundreds of sugar flowers or sprays.
- Fondant is much quicker than royal icing. To give a rough estimate, allow yourself one week to make a cake covered with fondant or ten days to complete a cake with royal icing—both with simple designs. Then allow one or two days for marzipanning and two days for making the cake.
- Remember that you can make some decorations in advance and store them carefully until use, which can save you some time.

- Before making a cake or icing, be sure you have the right ingredients for the recipe. Whether you measure by volume or weight, measure every ingredient carefully to ensure accuracy.

- Double-check the cake pan's size, measuring across its base if necessary. Pan sizes must match the recipe's quantities.

- Suggested cooking times are guidelines and are not exact. Always test the cake ten to fifteen minutes early and continue to bake the cake and test it at regular intervals until it is done.

- When marbling fondant, knead the leftover trimmings together to make one color and use it to cover the cake board.

- Mix leftover petal dust together and keep the mixture on hand for blending darker colors.

- Remember to coat cakes in a very thin layer of marzipan before covering them with royal icing.

- Allow royal icing to stand for a few minutes before assessing its consistency.

- When royal icing a cake smoothly, finish the top or the sides of the cake last, depending on the design. If the side of the cake is being seen and the top edge is piped, finish the sides last so that the top edge has the finish mark, or vice versa.

- Each time you apply a coat of royal icing to the top of a cake or the side of a round cake, finish at a different point each time to ensure that the cake is level on top and does not slope, the sides are even, and the cake is round, not lopsided.

- Before applying frills to the sides of a cake or piping extension work near the cake board, fit the ribbon or pipe the edging design first to prevent breakages.

- Piping extension work is very exacting. Pipe the lines of icing on different parts of the design instead of continuing all around the cake. If a thread breaks, it will take the wet threads of icing with it, but if the other threads have dried, only one thread will go.

Hygiene and Cleanliness

Special-occasion cakes are often admired by—and eaten by—many friends and family members at parties and celebrations. Therefore, it is essential to follow certain rules regarding hygiene, cleanliness, and using nonedible cake materials.

Bake and decorate cakes in a spotlessly clean environment. Use clean utensils, carefully prepared pans, and fresh ingredients. Scrub your hands, including under your fingernails, before starting. If you have any sort of cut or abrasion on your hands, cover the area well.

Wrap a fully baked cake well and store it in a clean, dry place to prevent mold growth. Brush the cake with apricot glaze before applying the marzipan to prevent any fermentation between the cake and the marzipan. Once you've covered the cake with marzipan and icing, store it on a new, clean cake board—used cake boards will harbor bacteria, especially in the score marks made when you cut the previous cake. Store the cake on the cake board in a new cardboard cake box in a dry place at all times. Keep the box closed during storage to prevent dust and other impurities from getting to the cake.

Here are some more tips:
- When covering a cake with royal icing or fondant, be sure that no small particles of dirt or cake crumbs get into the icing.
- Wear a white apron or cotton shirt so that fabric particles will not get into the icing or onto the work surface where you will be rolling out fondant.
- Always use white dishtowels and white cheesecloth so that colored specks will not get into the icing or on the cake.
- Apply all food colorings with clean toothpicks and throw them away afterward to prevent any contamination or color mixing.
- If you use any inedible decorations (including some types of food coloring and dust), label these pieces as inedible.

- Sugar flowers are usually made with floral wire and tape, stamens, and sometimes metallic colorings. Make it clear to the recipient of the cake that these types of decoration are definitely not edible.
- Always make wired flowers or work with any inedible materials on a separate work surface, away from finished cakes.
- Add pastillage and wired flower arrangements to the cake last and be sure to remove them before cutting the cake. These decorations may be kept as keepsakes, whereas molded decorations are often eaten.
- If using silk flowers, arrange them and secure them together so you can easily remove them from the cake.
- If using fresh flowers and leaves, choose only nonpoisonous varieties. If you are sugar-frosting fresh flowers, choose only edible flowers.
- Even though many gold and silver colorings and types of gold leaf are labeled as nontoxic, it is not wise to consume them.
- If you use pins to secure ribbons to cakes and cake boards, use stainless-steel pins with bead heads so you can easily see them. Also make sure that the cake's recipient knows that there are pins in or near the cake.

Assembling Cakes

Cakes iced with royal icing are easy to assemble because you place cake pillars directly on the cake and position them accordingly before placing the next cake on top. If you don't have the pillars in the right positions, you can lift up the cake and move the pillars. A cake looks better if the pillars are just underneath the corners of the top cake with the cake board proud of the pillars. If the pillars are too close to the center, the cake will look unbalanced.

To figure out the placement of the pillars for square cakes, cut out paper templates that are 2 inches (5 cm) smaller than the top of each cake. Fold the template into four and place the pillar on the open corner of the template. Draw around the pillar and cut out neatly. Open the template, place it on the center of the cake, and position the four pillars

on the cut spaces of the template. Remove the template and carefully position the next tier. On a round cake, it looks better to use three pillars, so use a round template and mark it in thirds to position the three pillars.

To assemble fondant cakes, you must use acrylic skewers with the pillars because the icing will not support the weight. Arrange the hollow cake pillars using the aforementioned template technique. Insert the skewers right through the icing into the cake until they are resting on the cake board. Mark the skewers level with the top of the pillars, carefully remove the pillars and skewers, and cut the skewers to the correct height. Replace the skewers and the pillars and position the cake.

A good guide to cake-tier spacing is to allow 2–3 inches (5–7½ cm) between each tier. The following sizes give a balanced appearance for a three-tiered cake:

5 + 7 + 9 inches (13 + 18 + 23 cm)

6 + 8 + 10 inches (15 + 20 + 25 cm)

6 + 9 + 12 inches (15 + 23 + 30 cm)

If the cake is going to have only two tiers, the distance between the tiers needs to be slightly greater to give a better balance: about 3 inches (7½ cm). The cake boards need to be 2–3 inches (5–7½ cm) larger than the cake to allow for the marzipan, icing, and decorations. Sometimes the size of the cake boards should be graduated to give a better balance; for example, 2 inches (5 cm) larger on the top tier, 3 inches (7½ cm) larger on the second tier, and 4 inches (10 cm) larger on the base tier. If the design is protruding over the edge of the cake, such as with run-out collars or extension work, allow extra room on the cake boards to prevent damage to the decorations.

Lining a Deep Cake Pan

For a rich fruitcake, use a good-quality fixed-base deep cake pan. Ensure you have the right pan size for the quantity of cake batter because this will affect both the depth and the baking time of the cake.

How to Line a Cake Pan

- Place the pan on double-thickness parchment paper and draw around the base. Cut out the marked shape with a pair of scissors.
- Cut a strip of double-thickness parchment paper long enough to wrap around the outside of the pan with a small overlap and to stand 1 inch (2½ cm) above the top of the pan.
- Brush the base and sides of the pan with shortening or oil. Place the cut-out shape in the base of the pan and press it flat. Place the double strip of paper inside the pan, pressing it well against the sides and making sharp creases where it fits into corners.
- Brush the base and side paper well with shortening or oil. Place a strip of double-thickness brown paper around the outside of the pan and tie it securely in place with string.
- Line a baking sheet with three or four layers of brown paper and stand the cake pan on top.

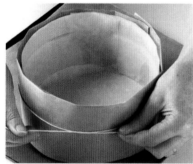

Did You Know?

When determining a cake pan's size, measure the pan across the base, not the top. To prepare the pan, double-line the inside of the pan with parchment paper and then the outside with double-thickness brown paper; this prevents the outside of the cake from getting overdone. When you put the cake in the oven, always stand the pan on a baking sheet lined with three or four thicknesses of brown paper to prevent the base from overbaking.

Templates

Several of the templates that appear on the next pages were used to create cake designs featured in the book; others are shown purely for inspiration. Copy and adapt the designs for your own cakes or modify them based on other sources of inspiration. If you want to use the templates at the size they appear in the book, simply trace the design onto tracing paper. However, you may need to enlarge or reduce the image to fit your cake, in which case the simplest way to do this by using a copier.

ABCDEFGHIJ
KLMNOPQRS
TUVWXYZ

ABCDEFGHIJKLMN
OPQRSTUVWXYZ

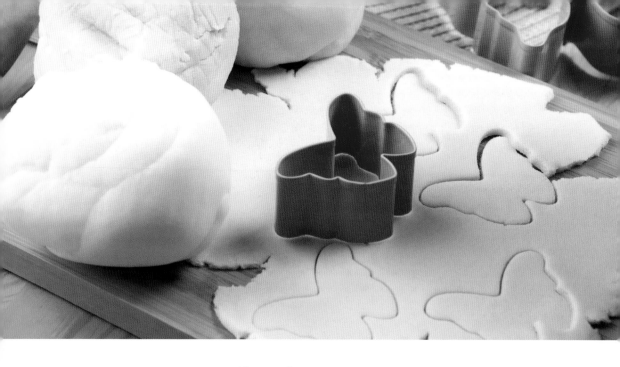

Index

Photo Credits

Front cover: Amawasri Pakdara/Shutterstock

Back cover: Amawasri Pakdara/Shutterstock

Spine: M. Unal Ozmen/Shutterstock

Title page: Amawasri Pakdara/Shutterstock

Banner graphic on chapter openers: Viktor Jarema/Shutterstock

Images by Chris Turner, with additional images from Shutterstock.com.

Illustrations by King & King Associates

138 (top); Malivan_Iulia, 23 (left); janecat, 62; JasminkaM, 18 (top [lace]); joannawnuk, 218; Normana Karia, 26 (top); klublu, 184 (bottom right); Ksju, 142; Magdalena Kucova, 12 (top); kuhn50, 87 (right), 89; Kuprevich, 34 (top); Andrei Kuzmik, 12 (bottom); lapas77, 179 (bottom right); Pelling Lee, 194 (bottom); Lestertair, 16; locrifa, 163; Lovely Bird, 13 (center); Lsa1978, 76 (bottom right); Sean MacD, 78 (top); madlen, 88 (border); rizal mansor, 14 (bottom); MaraZe, 92 (center), 177 (bottom right), 205; Mariontxa, 193 (top center); mayakova, 224; MDWines, 175; Irina Meliukh, 23 (center); Michael715, 49 (center); Monkey Business Images, 44 (bottom left), 46 (top), 58; Moolkum, 24 (bottom); My_inspiration, 83 (bottom); Ciprian Nasalean, 49 (left); Shmeliova Natalia, 74; Nattika, 36 (top); Naviya, 192 (bottom); Karin Nelson, 112 (top cake); ninikas, 23 (right), 25 (bottom), 33 (top); NoirChocolate, 28 (top); Nomad_Soul, 56; Oksana2010, 97 (top); Yakov Oksanov, 75 (bottom); Ermolaeva Olga 84, 19; Olyina, 104; M. Unal Ozmen, 116 (bottom right); Pacharawan, 64, 83 (center); Amawasri Pakdara, 2–3, 4, 9 (left), 54 (bottom right), 61 (top), 143 (right), 152 (top), 170; Daniela Pelazza, 72; Gary Perkin, 50 (top); Richard Peterson, 207 (top); pim pic, 31 (top); Praisaeng, 92 (top candy); qoppi, 110 (bottom); Quanthem, 90 (bottom); Rihardzz, 192 (center); Nestor Rizhniak, 39, 204; Roselynne, 5 (right); safakcakir, 18 (top [plate]); SamalMike, 100 (bottom); sashafolly, 43; EduardoSchmidt, 5 (left), 143 (left) , 146; Sellwell, 99 (bottom); Melnikov Sergey, 7 (top); Shebeko, 42 (bottom); Silatip, 140 (top right); simm49, 183 (bottom); sokolenok, 111 (top); Lori Sparkia, 144 (bottom), 147 (bottom); Sergio Stakhnyk, 25 (top); SpeedKingz, 143 (center); Pair Srinrat, 191 (left); Becky Starsmore, 40 (bottom); Stockcrafterpro, 119 (center); stockcreations, 98 (bottom right); Strannik_fox, 171 (left); Krystyna Taran, 122; tarttong, 207 (bottom); Joe Techapanupreeda, 171 (center); timquo, 7 (bottom), 147 (top), 208, 222; UfaBizPhoto, 37 (top), 191 (right); valkoinen, 133 (top); valzan, 110 (center left); Kurbatova Vera, 22; virtu studio, 86; wandee007, 79 (top); WORRAYUTH P, 103 (center); Naruedom Yaempongsa, 192 (top); yanami, 32; MAHATHIR MOHD YASIN, 112 (bottom swirl), 209; YKTR, 195 (top), 196; ZAHRA22, 6 (bottom)

About the Author

Janice Murfitt is respected home economist with professional experience in diverse areas of the food industry, including food styling, food writing and editing, nutrition, and baking, with particular expertise in cakes and cake decorating. She has worked with numerous prestigious international clients, including Nestle, Kraft, Unilever, General Mills, and Weight Watchers, and she has authored close to thirty cookbooks and food-related educational books.

Residing in London, England, Janice works with some of the UK's top food photographers, food stylists, advertising agencies, and production studios, lending her knowledge and vision to the creation of print ads and featured recipes and images for food magazines. Visit Janice's website at www.janicemurfitt.com.